Full of His Glory
Devotions from Nature

Written by:
Jana King James

Photography by:
Jana King James & David E. James

More nature photographs by Jana & David E. James may be viewed on-line and purchased at davidjphotoart.com.

All rights reserved by Jana King James © 2016.

Table of Contents

1. New You!
2. Winter Wonderland
3. The Ant
4. Dear God, Please…
5. The Bee
6. Mountain Movers
7. The Winds
8. Showers of Blessings
9. Metamorphosis
10. How to Get Wings
11. Do the Rocks Have to Cry Out?
12. Full of His Glory
13. Mountain Movers
14. Thunder Heads
15. Under the Blood
16. Consider the Lilies
17. Pound Puppy
18. The Harness
19. Floods
20. Wolves in Sheeps' Clothing
21. Weariness
22. Sonshine
23. Sunset
24. Flying Free
25. Reflections
26. Waves
27. Thick Skin
28. Sickness
29. Exercise
30. Pearls
31. All Washed Up
32. Birds of a Feather
33. Friendship
34. Rising to the Occasion
35. What You See Is What You Get
36. Living Water
37. You've Got to Have Heart
38. The Watchmen
39. Chimpanzees
40. Rainbow Promises
41. Eating Like a Hummingbird
42. Fog
43. Valleys
44. Stars
45. The Universe Sings His Praises
46. Colors of Autumn
47. Cardinals
48. The True Vine
49. The Sower
50. The Lion of Judah
51. The Sand Dollar
52. Trees
53. Fire!
54. The Lost Sheep
55. I Come to the Garden
56. Sunrise
57. Petrified Wood
58. The Serpent
59. Diamonds
60. Roots
61. Parenthood
62. Mature Fruit
63. Disk Flowers
64. Sand
65. Weeds
66. Rhinoceros
67. Morning Dew
68. Fragrance
69. Timing
70. The Golden Hour
71. Air
72. Variety
73. Roses
74. The Fragrance After the Rain
75. The Lamb of God
76. Sharks
77. The New Earth
78. Heaven
79. Ashes
80. The Harvest
81. Interdependency
82. Moonlight
83. Songbirds
84. Mimicry

Table of Contents (continued)

85. The River of Life
86. Spiritual Food
87. Organic Food
88. Geodes
89. Cultivation
90. Big Ducks on a Little Pond

Forward

In March, 2016, my husband, David, and I were led of the Lord to take a very brave step out of our comfort zone; we retired early from our jobs, sold our home of fifteen years and most of our possessions, and bought a motor coach in which to travel. We set out to see America and try to capture the beauty of God's creation through photography. Before leaving Texas, God spoke to me and told me that I was to write a devotion book about nature to show how biblical lessons can be learned from observing God's creation. After pointing out to the Lord that I had never written a book before, and I was merely a school teacher, He began to impress upon me that I had taught science from a Christian point of view for decades, and I preached countless chapel services and Bible classes over the years. So, I said, "Yes, Lord. I'm your servant, and I will do my best to follow your directions." I began writing this book in January, 2015. We took the photos used as illustrations between 2013 and 2016. It is my hope and prayer that you will gain ministry and encouragement from the devotions and photos contained in this book. Please let me know what you think or ask me any questions you may have by emailing me at jdkj0214@gmail.com. May God bless you and speak to you as you read this book!

1. New You!

"Old things are passed away. "…all things have become new." 2 Corinthians 5:17
Colossians 1:10&11; Ephesians 4:21-25

     "Happy New Year!" we say to each other on the first day of the year, but why then do we revert to old thoughts and habits that keep us imprisoned? Many plants, such as perennial hibiscus, die to the ground every winter. While the season is darker and colder than other seasons, it is the time when all the plant's energy is devoted to growing its roots deeper. Then, when spring comes, it is able to grow more and bigger branches and produce a multitude of blooms for everyone to see and enjoy.

     Are you allowing God to use the dark trials and challenges in your life to bring you closer to Him? When something is too much for you, go to the Word of God and let your roots grow deeper in faith? If you do, your spirit will become stronger in the Lord, and you will produce much spiritual fruit for the blessing and enjoyment of everyone around you. Make it your goal this year to give old detrimental things to God so that He can turn them into opportunities for growth. God can use what you learn from them as a blessing and ministry to you and those around you. Let God make you new and improved this year!

2. Winter Wonderland

"You are fearfully and wonderfully made." Palm 139:13-18; Matthew 10:29-31

Beautiful fluffy flakes take a leisurely path to the ground and make a magical glittering blanket of white draped elegantly over the landscape. One of my favorite things about changing seasons is the first snowfall of winter. All the white loveliness is the product of tiny individual six-sided flakes. Every one of them may have six sides, but if you are able to capture one and look at it under a magnifying glass, you will see something amazing! Every flake has its own uniquely special design. No two are exactly alike. Isn't it incredible that God can come up with so many different designs out of six-sided figures?

This is a great reminder to us that we, being much more important to God than snow, are unique and specially made. You are designed by God to triumphantly live your life to His glory. He has given you the talents, personality, appearance, and weaknesses that He knew would benefit your life most. He is the one who chooses when talents will be used in His service and when He will use your weaknesses to make you aware of your need for Him.

If you were to never born, there would be a hole in the fabric of human history which you were meant to fill. Ask God daily what His will is for your life. Let Him use you to accomplish those things that only you can. Listen to that still small voice as you go about your day, and follow His leading. Don't miss God's special assignment for you today.

3. The Ant

"Go to the ant, you sluggard…" Proverbs 6:6-8; Ecclesiastes 910; Philippians 3:12-14

      The ant is a very hard worker. It knows its place and its job in the ant colony and does its job with all its might. It doesn't wait to be told or directed by the other ants or the queen. It doesn't complain that its hard work isn't recognized or give up because the job is too hard or too boring. It is faithful to do the work until the end of its life. It doesn't try to suddenly be the queen, because it instinctively knows what its place is and stays without question.

      When God places an anointing on your life, or gives you a special calling, it is without repentance. We all have times when we get restless and want a change. We sometimes feel unappreciated or feel that what we are tasked to do isn't really important. Your boss may sometimes take the credit for the work you did or treat you unfairly. Perhaps, the promotion you've been working toward for years looks like it will never happen. These are the times when you put your eyes on God and remember that it is He who called you and opened this door for you. You do your work with excellence and integrity, knowing that it is the Lord who promotes in His good timing. Do everything you do as unto the Lord, because He is your real boss. He knows and sees everything you do. Be faithful until the end, and He will give you favor. Remember, if you are faithful in the small things, God will bless you with more important things.

4. Dear God, please…
"My God shall supply all my need according to His riches in glory, by Christ Jesus."
Philippians 4:19; Psalm 37:22-26; Luke 11:9-13

     In the winter time, birds have a difficult time finding food. People are encouraged to take bird feeding very seriously, because birds become dependent upon bird feeders when food is scarce. If those people forget to put food in them consistently, the birds could starve. People may not always be dependable, but in God's great provision, He designed many bushes and trees that produce berries which may be eaten all during the winter.

     This morning, I witnessed a wonderful sight! A brightly colored stellar jay came to the rock where we had placed dried fruit and nuts for the chipmunks and birds. He looked curiously at the pile of treats and carefully selected a peanut for himself. I was happy to see that we blessed one of God's creatures with a tasty morsel.

     God has many channels through which He can meet our needs. He may put it on the heart of one of His children to bless you in some way when you are in need. He may engineer circumstances which bring the answer in a round-about way. He may provide what you need seemingly out of thin air. I can say from personal experience that I have never gone without anything I truly needed. God has always been faithful.

     One year, we had so many unexpected expenses that we didn't have enough money to pay our very high property taxes. I asked the Lord to please provide some way. A few nights later, I heard a tremendous crash in our back yard. Our whole family went running to see what on earth had happened. A drunk driver had run her truck through one side of our fence, across our garden, through the other side of the fence, and into the side of our neighbor's house. No one was hurt! God found a very unusual way to provide the money we needed for taxes through insurance money. We fixed our fence, too!

     Trust God to provide what you need in His perfect timing. He never leaves His children begging for bread.

5. The Bee

"Promotion comes from the Lord." Psalm 75:5-7; Psalm 16:5-11; Galatians 6:7-10

    The bee, like the ant, instinctively knows what he should be doing. He goes from plant to plant collecting pollen to feed the colony and build the hive. The queen doesn't give him direct orders. He just knows what to do and does it.

    Many of us are so afraid that we will miss God's will for our lives that we don't do what we know to do. God expects us to provide for our families and pay our bills. It does not honor God if we don't and sit there saying that we are waiting on God for His direction about paying our bills. He has given us abilities and common sense to utilize to provide for our needs.

    If you are at a crossroads in your life, lay your life at His feet, and ask Him to open the right door in His perfect timing. Only do the things that give you peace in your spirit, but don't just sit there. Do what you know to do in the meantime. Don't make any hasty long-term decisions in the midst of chaos or confusion. God's way is the way of peace. Wait for God, and He will answer. He may use the very things you are doing in the interim to open the doors you have been waiting for, but remember to always follow after peace. That is where you will find God's leading.

6. Mountain Movers

"Say to the mountain, "Be cast into the sea, …" Matthew 17:19&20; Hebrews 11:1-6

God made mountains to be some of the largest and most impressive geographical features on the earth. They are usually made of solid rock and only erode slowly by weathering over a long period of time. They are formed to last as long as the earth does.

We have situations in our lives that look as tough and immense to us as mountains look. Humanly speaking, these problems look insurmountable and are here to stay; but as God's children, we do not have to live a life defeated by illness, conflict, doubt, worry, or any other persistent challenges.

God's Word is a powerful weapon. Many verses tell us to speak or say the Word of the Lord with confidence and authority. Because you are God's child, you have His Holy Spirit living in you and have the full authority and power of God at your command. You can speak God's words over all the bondages Satan may try to put on you. Claim God's promises in the name of Jesus. Thank the Lord for His answer and see it with spiritual eyes as being already done. Be willing to accept His perfect will, whether the answer is yes or no, and you will be the victor over the circumstance. If He says no, your situation is there to bring Him glory in some way and will bring eventual good in your life. Believe God's Word and walk by faith, not by sight. In God's perfect timing and perfect will, the answer will come. God always keeps His promises!

7. The Winds

"Do not be blown about by every wind of doctrine." Ephesians 4:14&15
Matthew 5:13; Psalm 19:7-11

Winds can be very powerful forces which can knock you off your feet. They can be 100-mile per hour straight line winds which flatten everything in their paths. They can be hurricanes, or tornadoes, which seem to pull you in every direction at once and leave you feeling confused and disoriented.

They can be beneficial winds. They can be refreshing breezes that revive your flagging body and soul. It can be that breath of freshness that cools your perspiring body on an otherwise warm and humid day. It is sometimes a welcome southern breeze that finally begins to blow after a long, cold winter.

The Bible tells us to be wary of winds of doctrine. There seem to be fads and new teachings, young prophets and preachers, new books, and new strategies popping up all the time in Christian circles. We are constantly bombarded by the media with what THEY think is acceptable or politically correct. The world would prefer that we Christians blend in and take a "We are the world" mentality. As we become more worldly, our ability to bring people to Christ is weakened.

Believers, stay in the Word. Keep God's laws ever before you. Don't allow the world and its doctrines to dilute the Gospel of Christ and the Scriptures. Be the salt of the earth you are called to be, and don't be afraid to stand up for Christ and godliness. There is something wrong with the Church if the world is comfortable with us. We are doing something right when the devil is bringing great opposition against us. Are worldly people always comfortable around you? Are you at home around them?

8. Showers of Blessings

"Let patience have her perfect work…" James 1:2-4; Ephesians 1:3

     In the water cycle, as the sun shines down on the earth, water molecules become more active; they rise into the air becoming water vapor. As it rises higher into the sky, the water vapor hits tiny pieces of dust and other particles and combines with it to form bigger and bigger drops. As they continue to rise, they cool and stick together and form a cloud. Soon the droplets become too large to remain in the air and fall as rain sleet, or snow.

     In my prayer times, I find myself asking God to send a shower of blessings to me or someone else. When I pray this way, I am just asking for God's blessings and not thinking about the process which creates a shower. I should not be surprised by the rising of issues and complications in my life that are God's way of producing the showers I have asked for. I see what I want, and God sees what I need to learn before He can impart to me those blessings. He allows clouds of problems to overshadow me until I learn from them what I need to learn, then God can release the rain of blessings on my life that this new wisdom has prepared me to handle wisely.

9. Metamorphosis

"But be ye transformed by the renewing of your mind." Romans 12:2;
2 Corinthians 4:15-18; Acts 14:21&22

    For the past several years, my husband and I have been building a butterfly garden. As avid photographers, we love to capture the beauty of one of the loveliest of God's creations in photos. Last spring, for the first time, we attempted to rescue caterpillars from being eaten by wasps. They were helpless targets out in the open, providing a large tasty meal for wasps on the hunt. We placed them in enclosures with the correct host plant and watched over them carefully. All they did was eat. They shed their old skins several times before finally crawling up to the top of the container, attaching themselves to the top in a jay position, and becoming chrysalises. There they would remain for around ten days or more. When one was fully developed, it pushed itself out of its casing.

Upon emerging, its wings were all shriveled up and its body appeared fat. It had to hang upside down until all the liquid it had stored in its body flowed into the veins in its wings and pumped them up and out from the body. In a few hours, the wings had straightened out and hardened. Then the butterfly flew away to enjoy its life.

    This metamorphosis is a great lesson in being born again. When a person first comes to Christ, he is like that little caterpillar who needs to constantly be fed the Word of God and is extremely vulnerable to the enemy. He needs to be sheltered by fellow believers and mentored while still a baby Christian. It is our responsibility, when we lead someone to Christ, to make sure they know to read the Word daily so they can be transformed into the image of Jesus Christ. When we have the mind of Christ, we will be filled with the Holy Spirit and be enabled to fulfill His special calling on our lives and fight enemies on our own, with the help of the Holy Spirit. Let us all be transformed by the Word of God today and become new creatures in Christ Jesus!

10. How to Get Wings

"They that wait upon the Lord shall renew their strength…" Isaiah 40:31; Exodus 15:2

Their powerful wings enable them to soar and glide at tremendous heights while hunting their prey and have the ability to descend at great speed to pluck a swimming fish right out of the water. They make it look so easy when they effortlessly pick up a field mouse they spotted from hundreds of feet above the ground. Such strength and ability has been gifted to eagles.

The Word of God says that when we wait upon the Lord, our strength will be renewed as the eagles. We will be able to fly through the tasks of our day without becoming weary or fainting. The key is to wait upon the Lord. Sometimes we tend to run ahead of God in eagerness to get things done. In doing so, we get tired or discouraged and fail to complete the job. We all need to wait for God's timing. When we do, things come together with much less effort. With the anointing and blessing of God, He goes before us and with us, making all things work together for our success. Stay in the will of God and your efforts will be rewarded.

11. Do the Rocks Have to Cry Out?

"If we do not praise Him, the very stones are going to cry out." Luke 19:37-40; Psalm 34:1-4

    All of creation points us to the Creator. His workmanship is evident in trees, mountains, and rocks. These things have a purpose of being all their own. They are to provide food, oxygen, and shelter for other living things. We don't think of them in terms of having hands or voices.

    The Bible tells us that we are made to give praise to our Father God and fellowship with Him. We are to praise Him at all times, on good days and bad. His praise should continually be in our mouths. This is one of the commands we see in Psalms, "Praise the Lord!" Why? We need to praise God because when we are not praising and thanking God, we can easily fall into Satan's traps of depression, anger, and self-pity. When we have thankful hearts, we drive away negative attitudes and thoughts that can take away our joy and faith. The Scriptures also say that if we don't praise Him, then the rocks will cry out. That's not their job. Let's give praise to God today, and give the rocks a break!

12. Full of His Glory

"The whole earth is full of His glory." Isaiah 6:3; Exodus 34:29-31

    To me, it is an awe-inspiring experience to see visible rays which come down to hit the ground like golden curtains, bringing the day to a close. I relate such shining to God's glory. Moses was allowed to see God's presence, so God's glory must involve a brightness or glow.

    On occasion, I have been told that my face had a glow about it. I remember a particular time when getting acquainted with someone while working. I said something about the Lord, and the coworker said she knew I was a Christian because she could see it in my face.

    People shouldn't have to look at the sky to see God's shining glory reflected by the sun. The Father has many "sons" from which His glory should be shining, because they have recently spent time in the presence of Almighty God. Are people able to bask in the glow from your face today? Set aside time to spend alone with god daily. Let your light shine!

13. Mountain Tops

"I will lift up mine eyes to the hills- from whence cometh my help?" Psalm 121:1-3
John 6:3

    When I really want to be as close to God as I can get, my heart yearns for the mountains. There is something about being up high on a mountain that makes me feel as though I am in one of god's most sacred temples. It is as if I am high above all the regular ordinary aspects of life where I am able to look down upon it with a clear perspective, and I rejoice that I can be out of the busyness and chaos of daily monotonous routines and problems. I can finally be in a place of joy, peace, and rest where it is possible to recharge and be renewed in my spirit.

    Unfortunately, mountain tops are not usually places where God intends us to live and remain. High mountains are bare of tall trees and most plant growth. Just like those plants we grow best and tallest down on the hills and in valleys. God gives us mountain top experiences so we can gain His perspective on our challenges and prepare us for our next growing experience. We all need to learn to love the valleys as much as the mountains, because in the valleys we grow to be more like Jesus.

14. Thunder Heads

"Whatever a man thinks in his heart, so is he." Proverbs 23:7a; Ephesians 4:30-32

      Some clouds are beautiful airy cirrus clouds which can be seen through and contain tiny dimensional ice crystals. Stratus clouds blanket everything in fog and deliver a steady light rain. Cumulus clouds are big puffy cotton balls which hold lots of moisture, and when they are full of water droplets too heavy to hold, they turn gray and send down heavy rain. Sometimes they are buffeted by such strong winds that the droplets are pulled back up to the cloud over and over freezing them. The droplets turn into pieces of hail which finally become too heavy and plummet to the ground, leaving destruction in their wake. These cumulonimbus clouds can become so agitated that they begin to rotate and send down tornadoes which can devastate whole towns when colliding with the ground.

      Just as clouds can hold water in various ways, people can hold things inside them. Things like anger, grudges, grief, sin, hate, and depression. The longer those things are held inside, the more agitated a person becomes. If these things take hold in his heart, they begin to affect what is coming out of him and how he is perceived by others. Eventually, if these issues are not dealt with appropriately, they will come spewing out and rain destruction on everyone he encounters.

      We all need to keep our hearts right with God and each other. We shouldn't allow these ungodly attitudes to set up residence in our hearts and minds. Give them to God, get right with others, and forgive. Let's not be thunder heads!

15. Under the Blood

"He was wounded for our transgressions. He was bruised for our iniquities. The chastisement of our peace was upon Him, and by His stripes we are healed." Isaiah 53:5;
Hebrews 9:22; Matthew 26:28; I Peter 1:18&19

      The dogwood flower has a powerful story to tell. It has four petals in the shape of a cross. The tip of each petal is tinged with red. It is yet another picture from nature of what Jesus has done for us. This red color on each of the four petals reminds us of the blood Jesus shed for our sins from His head, hands, and feet while on the cross.

      Some people don't like to think about the blood of Christ because they think of it as gruesome or gory. It is difficult to think of all that Jesus Christ endured in order to save us and give us eternal life. The blood that He shed was essential payment for our salvation. He was the spotless Lamb of God, the only one capable of taking away the sins of all mankind. Without the shedding of innocent blood, there would be no payment for sin, and all the world would be forever lost. That blood has the power to cover all sin: past, present, and future. Otherwise, we who are alive today could not be saved. As Andre Crouch wrote in one of his songs, "The blood that gives me strength from day to day, it will never lose its power!" Thank God for the blood of Jesus!

16. Consider the Lilies

"Consider the lilies of the field, they do not toil…" Matthew 6:25-34;
Philippians 4:13

    Lilies come in so many shapes, colors, and sizes. There are countless beautiful wildflowers which appear in the landscape every spring. No one plants or waters or feeds them. They just grow up and bless us with their loveliness. They are given everything they need by the Heavenly Father. They don't work for water and food and a place to live. It is all provided for them.
    Worry is a sin. It is, in effect, saying to God and others who are watching, "I don't really believe God can take care of me, my problems, or my needs. I have to figure out solutions all by myself. God doesn't really love me." While we should use the brain God gave us to figure out day to day things, we should always take everything that concerns us and lay it all at Jesus' feet. We are not to come back and pick it up later to worry about it some more. Leave it with God and begin thanking Him for the answer. Then God will freely give us what He sees that we need. Trust God with your life today!

17. Pound Puppy

"We are joint heirs with Christ…" Romans 8:14-17; Ephesians 1:4-14

    One day, at the end of June, 2010, my husband voiced his desire to me to have a new dog. He was at home recovering from heart surgery and in need of a companion to help fill his time while recuperating. I readily agreed and began searching on-line for a border collie puppy which we were interested in having. As hard as I tried, I couldn't find a single one available. I began to pray and asked the Lord to help us find a wonderful little lap dog to be a part of our family. I was suddenly impressed in my spirit that we should visit our local animal shelter to see what they had available. I told my husband about my idea and he immediately agreed. When we arrived, we made the circuit past all the kennels and didn't really connect with any of the dogs. We went around a second time. This time, I noticed a long very skinny little black dog with four white feet and a white chest standing at the window next to me. I held out my hand to say hi and she licked the glass where my hand was. We had them bring her out, along with two others. She instantly melted our hearts with her sweetness and gentle, but spunky, nature. Because of her love for giving kisses, we named her Kissy. She has been a part of our family for five years now. We love her like she was our own daughter and can't imagine our lives without her. She is ours!

    When we were saved, our Heavenly Father adopted us into His family and gave us all the rights and privileges that His heirs have. If we can love our pets that we adopt so much, how much more does our Heavenly Father love us as His adopted children? Today, meditate on the love your Father has for you and how much He enjoys fellowship with you. Talk with Him much and often. Let Him know how much you love Him, and thank Him for making you a part of His family.

18. The Harness

"Lead me and guide me…" Psalm 31:1-5; Psalm 25:9&10

      Our dog, Kissy, loves to go on walks! If we get busy with something else in the afternoon, she will come and sit in front of us and stare at us. If that doesn't work she will start sneezing or whining to get our attention. We put a harness on her when we take her out. We use a harness because it wraps around her middle and shoulders to protect her neck from being damaged if she pulls hard against the leash. A lot of the time she doesn't need it. She will walk contentedly beside us, and the leash is lax. If she doesn't stay with us, the harness begins to tighten on her body. When she tries to dart out in the street, we pull very hard on the leash to get her quickly out of danger. The harness is there to keep her safe and out of danger.

      When we are born again, God fills us with His Holy Spirit. He walks with us and is our Helper and our Guide. When we are walking in God's will, we feel free and at peace. But when we are making bad decisions, we feel a tug in our spirits that cautions us not to do that. When we are violating God's will for our lives or are in danger, we get a sense of deep dread warning us to stop immediately and seek the Lord's will. The Holy Spirit is a wonderful counselor, friend, protector, and guide. Be sensitive to the leading of the Holy Spirit and learn to follow it. He will never steer you wrong.

19. Floods
"The floods shall not overflow you…" Isaiah 43:2; Isaiah 44:3

    It's spring! The snow has begun to melt. The temperatures have begun to warm. There are little bits off green peeking out of all the plants and trees. There is a hint of freshness in the air. The region is waking up from its winter sleep. In the midst of all this loveliness also comes flooding, All the snow from the mountains and hills begins to melt at once and water pours from every crack and crevice, joining forces in streams and rivers, overflowing banks, and taking with it rocks and silt from upstream. Floods can reach neighboring towns and uproot trees and houses. These are the things we usually think of when someone mentions floods.

    There are also benefits that come from floods. In ancient times, Egypt depended on and welcomed the yearly flooding of the Nile River. The flood waters would bring with them fertile top soil which would be deposited on the river's banks. These banks would be sowed with food crops and be harvested to provide food for the Egyptians for the entire year. Without the floods, the soil would be overworked and produce much less for that year,

    Floods come into our lives, and all we tend to see is the destruction it brings. If we step back and look at them with spiritual eyes, what has been lost has out-lived its usefulness or is something we really don't need in our lives at all. What is left in your life when the waters recede is the fertile soil of a lesson learned, a place where fruit is produced to feed the soul and be shared with others. Without this result being realized, the flood's purpose would be lost and the experience would have to be repeated later until we learn the desired lesson. When floods come, let them do their good works and make fertile soil in you, where the fruit of the spirit can grow and ripen.

20. Wolves in Sheeps' Clothing

"He that dwells in the secret place of the most high…" Psalm 91

Wolves are beautiful animals. They remind us of our sweet loyal pets who in the same genus of the animal kingdom. They are tremendous hunters and often work with their pack in order to kill large prey. They are cunning in the way they scout out the smallest or weakest, sneak up on them, and attack. God gave them these instincts so they can have the ability to get food and survive.

A while back, I had been in a job I really liked for eight years. I liked my boss and the people with whom I worked. We mutually respected each other. The problem came when the administration removed my boss and his assistant and put in new ones. The new boss said she was a Christian, a pastor's wife, and smiled and gave lots of hugs to people, but there was something about her that just didn't seem genuine. As time went on, she began to accuse people of things and make things more and more difficult for the staff. I was beginning to see her smile to people's faces and then try to get ammunition on them when they weren't around. There was no real fruit of the Spirit coming from her. Her witness became one of judgment and destruction.

Beware of wolves in sheep's clothing. The Word says to judge the spirits and that we will know real believers by their fruit. This person proved herself to be false by her actions and the way she treated others.

When you are attacked by people like this, remember that God is your strength, your refuge, and your defender. His children will always come out on top. Just trust Him and give Him all your battles. He will protect you. He will make sure that the truth will win out in the end, even when it looks like you have been defeated by the wolves.

21. Weariness
"The Lord is my shepherd…" Psalm 23

There are times that I have given and given, worked myself really hard, been stressed out, and felt like I just fought a war. I just have nothing left and wish I could take a time out from life. I get a longing in my spirit to just pack a bag and leave and go somewhere restful where I can find peace again.

One of my favorite places to go is beside a stream. One that runs through a great forest of trees full of wildlife. I like to find a big log or rock on which to sit next to the water. I close my eyes and listen to the sounds of the water gently trickling downstream while the birds add harmony with their cheerful chirping. A peace and a calm comes over me. The rat race of life seems to gradually fade into the distance assuming its proper proportions once again. The Holy Spirit begins to speak to me and give me comfort, strength, and renewal. I become energized to resume my life and return home.

You may not be able to always go to a physically quiet place when you need one, but you can find a place in your home and shut the door. Get alone with God and take a drink of the living water of the Holy Spirit. Restore your soul by reading the Bread of Life. Talk to your Father and let Him love you and encourage you. He will always be with you when you call. He is always waiting to spend time with you. Give Him time regularly, and let the stress melt away. He loves you! He is for you!

22. Sonshine

"The light shines in the darkness, but the darkness did not comprehend it."
John 1:4&5 Matthew 5:14-16; Matthew 13:43

    Have you ever watched the news on television and wondered to yourself, "Why can't people see how wrong that is? Why do they want to continue in something that is so bad for our country? Don't they see what's going on?" The answer is no.

    The Bible says, "We walk in the light as He is in the light." Christians can see things clearly because of the light of the Holy Spirit that we abide in daily. The Word also says the light shines in the darkness, and the darkness could not understand it. The unsaved people of this world are moving about in darkness. The Bible tells us that they have scales on their eyes and are blinded to the truth. It is impossible for the lost to see because the prince of darkness has control over them. We need to continually pray for our lost world, and make ourselves available to witness to them. The only true light they can see comes from the children of God. Don't hide your light under a bushel. The world needs a lot more sonshine!

23. Sunset

"He gives us songs in the night…" Job 35:10; I John 1:5-7; Psalm 30:5

Sunset is a very magical time of day. Suspended between night and day, are glorious hues of yellows, pinks, oranges, purples, and blues. Sometimes rays of light can be seen streaking from behind stray clouds, Sometimes the horizon takes on a burning glow as though someone has taken a match to it, and the clouds on the opposite sky turn a vivid pink and purple. As the sky continues to darken, the bright colors turn to subdued blues and deep purples, trailing off into darkness. The day has ended, and the night has come.

The darkness is comforting, but also a bit scary. In the absence of light, we can't see what is coming or where we are going. When the light dawns, then we can see the start of a new day.

This process is just like life. God puts us on a path when the sun is shining brightly. It may rain a challenge or two on us, but if we are in God's will, we know that we should continue on. Eventually, our path forks in two directions or come to dead ends, then we don't know which way we should go. The sun sets and we feel lost and alone in the dark.

It is then that we need to call on the One True Light to shine on our life's path and help us to find the path to His will for the next chapter in our lives. While we wait in the darkness, God will give us a song and fellowship with us to prepare us for the dawn of the new day, or chapter of life, we are about to enter. You are not leaving the good times of life behind, just walking into the new experiences ahead that God is preparing for you. Night is not the end; it is a time of rest before a new beginning. "Weeping may come for a night, but joy comes in the morning!"

Life is full of endings and new beginnings. When God is doing a new thing, don't be afraid. Keep your eyes on the sunrise! All earthly things end; it's just a part of life.

24. Flying Free

"In everything give thanks..." I Thessalonians 5:16-18

As I shared with you earlier, we had a butterfly garden in our backyard. Many of the plants died in the winter, and we tried to put plants that need winter shelter in our greenhouse to keep them from dying. After the plants had all been arranged and everything cleaned up, we discovered that the last monarchs which came through the garden had left us caterpillars. We decided to let them grow and just live out their lives in the greenhouse. Time went by, and they emerged and were lovely perfect monarch butterflies. We were so excited about butterflies in December! We had lots of flowers in the greenhouse from which they could sip delicious nectar. We put out little bowls of wet sand for them and had warm bright grow lights in which they could bask.

Unfortunately, the butterflies were not impressed. They didn't want to eat or explore the greenhouse. They didn't want to drink anything. They weren't interested in anything in the lovely, safe, warm greenhouse. They just went to the windows and proceeded to run into them over and over, trying to get outside. They could see the sun and blue sky, and their instincts kept whispering to them, "You need to be out there flying free!" The first ones continued this behavior until they died on the window sill.

The second group came along. This time, even though chances were slim that they would make is to Mexico before freezing, we let them go after a few days. We didn't know what happened to them, but we hoped they made it.

These butterflies are just like us. God puts us in a safe, warm environment where we can be fed and grow until He is ready for us to fly. Instead of taking advantage of what we have now and enjoying it, we complain about our lack of freedom and how we want to be somewhere else. Trust God that He knows what is best for us and knows when it's time for us to branch out. Don't rush into responsibilities you aren't ready for. Let God lead you out at the right time, and He will bless your ministry and efforts.

25. Reflections

"Whatsoever things are true…" Philippians 4:8&9; Psalm 19:13&14

    My husband and I love to go to the national parks in Wyoming. There are magnificent vistas around every corner. If you are blessed to be in the right places at the right times, you can capture fantastic photographs where the water on the lakes is perfectly still and becomes like a mirror. We took some amazing pictures of the Tetons reflected perfectly on the surface of these lakes.
    In order for this to happen, the light has to hit the object by the water at just the right angle in order to then reflect its image on the lake. If the sun is not right or if there is any wind or disturbance in the water, there is no reflection.
    If we are to be reflections of Jesus and His love, we must first be in His presence. Only what you are close to, are you able to reflect. We must, in our hearts, be constantly before the Lord and consciously seek His presence. We must be careful not to let ripples of distractions, conflict, or anger blur the reflection of Jesus in us. Most assuredly, we cannot let the winds of Satan and sin completely take away His reflection in us.
    The word reflection also means the act of thinking about, or meditation on something. To exude the love of Jesus, we should be meditating on His words and practicing His presence in our lives at all times, whether actively or in our spirits. In doing this, we can be a perfect reflection of Jesus to those around us.

26. Waves

James 1:5-8

Children of God are not meant to be tossed about by the waves of life's trials like a sea shell caught in the ocean's waves. When a storm comes up and the seas get rough, we should not be swift to break out the life boats and abandon ship.

We have a Life Preserver. We have Someone who always is alert to our calls for help. Our Father never puts on us more than we can bear. He not only wants us to be at peace and have faith that we will be rescued, but He wants us to even be willing to step out of the boat and onto the waves if He tells us to.

We must learn to walk by faith and not by sight. Faith is what turns those things we don't yet have into reality. It is the stuff from which miracles are made.

What is in your heart today? Faith or doubt? Are you sinking, swimming, or walking on those waves? Peter walked on that water; Jesus slept through that storm at sea. What do you choose to do?

27. Thick Skin

"If you have something against your brother…" Matthew 5:21-24; Proverbs 18:21; Proverbs 12:18; James 4:11; Hebrews 4:12

    A rhinoceros has very thick skin, several inches in fact. His skin protects him from enemy attacks and serious injury. It also helps regulate his body temperature in the extreme temperatures.
    As Christians, we sometimes have very thin skin. We allow anything, however small, that someone might say to wound us. We carry around resentment, hurt, and anger against the offender for sometimes months and even years. The tragedy is that most of the time the offender isn't even aware that they hurt anyone. The wounded person is responsible for all the damage he has inflicted on himself through unforgiveness and bitterness.
    We also need to guard what we say ourselves, making sure that what we have to say is constructive and helps to correct or build up the other person with a spirit of love.
    Our words are as powerful as a two-edged sword. Always choose them wisely, and look carefully at the intent of your heart. Pray and ask the Lord to give you the right words and attitude before you speak. If it isn't edifying, don't say it. Also, develop a thick skin, and don't allow what others say to cause you to stumble in your Christian walk. Be slow to anger and quick to forgive. Develop a thick skin.

28. Sickness

"…By His stripes we are healed." Isaiah 53:4&5; James 5:14-16; Matthew 18:19

There are many reasons for plants to get sick and die. They may contract mold or mildew; they might get aphids or spider mites on them; they could be attacked by nematodes, eaten by caterpillars, get black spot, or root rot. When they get sick, they don't look well. Sometimes they turn yellow or lose their leaves. You can tell by its outward appearance that it's sick and will die if someone doesn't take steps to bring healing to the plant.

When people get sick, it can be caused by many different things. We may catch a virus from someone or be lacking in rest or nutrition. It can also be brought on by a root of bitterness in our spirits. No matter what the source of the illness is, God is our Great Physician. There is nothing He is unable to heal. Nothing is impossible with Him! Because of the stripes Jesus took for us, we are healed. Many verses of Scripture tell us about the Lord's power to heal. We all need to stand on God's Word and believe Him for our healing. God has many ways of healing. He knows what is best for us. We should do our part to bring it about, and He will do the rest!

29. Exercise

"Be strong and take heart..." Psalm 31:24; Hebrews 12:12-14;

II Timothy 4:5-8; Jude 20-25

Butterflies are constantly flying around from place to place. Always looking for some tasty pollen...or a mate! Animals get plenty of exercise and don't even have to wonder if they're getting enough of it to stay healthy, but people are another story.

I am the world's worst about regular exercise! I know I need to do it, but I am all ready with excuses why I can't do it right now. The muscles of the body must have regular use, or else they eventually will waste away. It has also been proven that if we don't use our minds, we will lose the sharpness and good memories we now have.

God wants us to be strong in Him and in the power of His might. He wants us to be able to run and not be weary and walk and not faint, both physically and spiritually. We need to exercise our faith. Through many answered prayers, our faith is built up. We can believe God and have faith for greater and greater things. God needs strong prayer warriors who have the faith to believe Him to move the spiritual mountains we are facing in this world. God is looking for those saints who are willing to still believe Him in the face of all the worldly giants we're fighting today. Stand and fight, Church! Satan may win some battles, but Jesus Christ has already won the war.

30. Pearls

"Do not cast your pearls before swine…" Matthew 7:6; Matthew 13:45&46

Pearls are the sea's precious treasures. They come in many shapes, sizes, and colors. It is quite interesting how they come to be. It all starts with an oyster sitting on the ocean floor. It decides to open up its shell for just a moment and a grain of sand settles inside its shell. It feels a little prick of discomfort and secretes a substance which coats the sand. It continues to coat the sand over and over until it is smooth. At the end of this process, a beautiful pearl has been produced. Not every oyster has a pearl inside. Some live out their lives never producing a single pearl.

When God puts irritants and challenges in our lives, they are meant to make us learn lessons and mature us into soldiers of the cross. Those lessons are like badges of honor, treasures, pearls of great price. We don't come by them easily. It takes lots of work, time, and grief to attain them. That is why we must be wise about when and with whom we share our pearls of wisdom. Only share them when God directs. Some people will only throw them in the garbage and not learn anything from your experience. Those are the ones who have to learn the hard way. Pray for them. Ask God to help them to learn for themselves and not miss out on their own precious pearls. Be ready to share with them when they are ready to hear.

31. All Washed Up

"God sent angels to Elijah and said, 'What are you doing here...'" I Kings 19:9-16

Waves are interesting. The wave is actually a disturbance that is going through the water. When it has passed, the water goes back to its original place, but any small objects that were caught up in the wave get left on the shore and are at the mercy of any other waves which come along to bring them back into the ocean. If they are covered by too much sand, they are stuck on the beach, and can never go back.

You may be feeling like a little shell on the beach today- all washed up. Life can be brutal sometimes, and because you are only human, you may be feeling depressed and sorry for yourself. The devil may be whispering to you that you are worthless, nobody cares, and you might as well just stop trying.

The great Old Testament prophet, Elijah, had that experience. Ahab and Jezebel were trying to kill him after he had called fire down from Heaven. He got scared and ran away. He sat down under a broom tree and asked God to let him die. Eventually, he fell asleep from sheer exhaustion. God didn't chastise Elijah for running away. He knew Elijah was overwhelmed by all he had just been through. God sent an angel to wake him, feed him, and give him another assignment. The angel asked him what he was doing there. Elijah, after his human needs had been met, realized he needed to go back and continue doing God's work.

If you are in this place in your life, don't just give up. Sometimes you just need some sleep, quiet, nourishment, and to talk to the Lord; He still loves you! He cares about how you are feeling. Be still before God, and let Him minister to you. He will refresh you and heal your wounded, washed-up spirit. When it is time, get back in the water of life. Don't allow the devil to keep you washed ashore and lying on the beach. Your job isn't finished yet!

32. Birds of a Feather

"He sets the solitary in families..." Hebrews 10:24&25; Acts 2:42-45;

Ps. 68:5&6

Many kinds of birds travel in flocks. Lots of other animals travel in groups, too. There are many reasons why God put them in groups: for protection, to help raise their young, to encourage mating, etc. They play together, eat, sleep, travel, and even mourn together. Some birds have a mate for life, while others don't.

We were not made to be alone either. In the beginning, God created Adam and Eve to be together and have a family. In the New Testament, God commanded the church not to neglect coming together. We are to fellowship with other believers regularly, even if just with your spouse. We need the friendship and encouragement of like-minded people. Others need what you have to offer as well.

In the body of Christ, we are all given gifts which we are to use for the benefit of the church and sometimes for unbelievers. Without regular fellowship, the body becomes disjointed and can't function in the way it was designed. Whether it is going out to eat with friends or family, participating in a home fellowship, or attending a church service, we should not distance ourselves from other believers. None of us are perfect, including pastors. We all make mistakes. Don't use being hurt as an excuse to keep you from fellowship with other Christians. Many people fellowship in home groups rather than a traditional church. Stay in the flock where there is food, protection, fellowship, help, and love. Fellowship happens anywhere and everywhere two or more believers are gathered together. Find a flock and stay connected!

33. Friendship

"There is a friend that sticks closer..." Proverbs 18:24; Matthew 26:35-40;

Proverbs 17:17

These two elephants seem to really love each other. Just before this picture was taken, their trunks were intertwined. They ate together and walked around together. They seemed inseparable.

Everyone needs a good friend. My mom used to tell me, "To have a friend, you must show yourself friendly." Good friends are hard to come by. If you are in need of a good friend, try being one first. Be a good listener. Make yourself available to help when someone is in need. Be willing to give your time to be with someone. Put others first. Be cheerful and upbeat. BE a friend. You'll soon have many friends.

Sometimes we have many friends, and we still feel alone. The Word tells us that Jesus is a friend who sticks closer than a brother. He is always there for us. He listens, He cares, He helps, He advises, He protects, and He is always with us. We are never alone! We can always count on Him.

34. Rising to the Occasion

"…God's way is perfect…" Psalm 18:30-36; Hebrews 13:20&21

Many fish have organs called swim bladders. They are little balloon-like structures which contain air. When the fish wants to be close to the surface of the water, he puts more air in his swim bladder so that he can maintain that depth with very little effort as long as he likes. If he desires to dive down deeper, he releases the air from his swim bladder.

When God calls you to perform a specific task, you don't need to worry that you can't do it. If you simply trust the Lord, He will give you the level of anointing that you need, through His Holy Spirit, to be successful in that task. He will always equip you for jobs He assigns to you. He will not, however, anoint you to perform jobs which He did not assign to you. If you walk in His will, you will be successful. But if you choose to do what God didn't call you to, you will ultimately fail. Always seek to rise to the occasion of following God's leading, and you will, with the help of the Holy Spirit, rise to the level of God's blessing and success.

35. What You See Is What You Get

"Whatsoever things are pure..." Philippians 4:8&9

I find it uplifting to see all the colorful spring flowers beginning to open along with the new season. The air is crisp with a hint of coming warmth. The sun is bright in the sky. There is a sense of freshness. Everything seems new and budding with possibilities. Others looking on that same scene may describe it very differently. They may find so many colors bunched together garish and too busy. They may complain that the weather is getting too warm, or that the harsh sun is going to give them sunburns. They may be getting stuffed up noses and gripe about the pollen in the air making them have allergy problems.

The Bible tells us to focus on the positive things. Talk about what is good. Find encouraging things to say. What can you praise God for today? What have you been blessed with? If you think that you are going to have a bad day, then chances are, you will. If you let one bad thing that happens at the beginning of a day determine the rest of the day, then it will. Choose to make this day be a good one. Set your mind on good and positive things. Choose happiness and thankfulness. What you choose to see in this day is the kind of day you will get.

36. Living Water

"...Out of his heart shall flow rivers..." John 7:38; Revelation 21:6

Water is so refreshing! The sound of waves rushing up on shore, brooks babbling over pebbles, and rivers tumbling down waterfalls, have the ability to soothe raw nerves and quiet the mind. When a person is thirsty, there is nothing that can replace a cool drink of pure water. Without water, nothing on earth could exist. Our bodies are over three fourths water, and most of the earth is covered by it.

The Bible speaks a lot of "living water." The living water the Bible refers to is the Holy Spirit. We need to drink Him in daily. Our spirit has a thirst that can only be quenched by being filled with the Holy Spirit. In the New Testament, we are commanded not to be drunk with wine, but instead be filled with the Holy Spirit.

It is true that Jesus once turned water into wine, and people drank wine in the Bible. They had to put wine into the water in order to decontaminate it so it could be drunk. The fine wine of Bible times was much lower in alcohol content than the wine of today.

Many people today are accustomed to having a glass of wine with dinner, but that is not getting drunk. In our day and age, we are surrounded by a society that doesn't know how to have a good time without alcohol. Everywhere we look, we are encouraged to buy beer and wine. If you tell someone you don't drink, they look at you like you are an alien. What a shame that even some of today's Christians are out getting drunk on Friday or Saturday night and showing up at church to repent on Sunday, and they think that's okay. There are more and more alcoholics every day because of peer pressure and this worldly mindset.

Wake up children of God! We are to be separate from the world- a peculiar people that are charged to call the lost world out of darkness and into the light. Seek the Holy Spirit and the kingdom of God. Follow after holiness and righteousness, and satisfy your thirsty soul with Living Water. Don't dim your light with worldly excesses. Let the Living Water flow from you and make you a world-changer.

37. You've Got to Have Heart

I Corinthians 13

A palm tree has some similarities to a person. They both have limbs and trunks, they both have types of outer skins, and they both have hearts. A person has layers of skin, while a palm tree has layers of bark. A palm's heart is called the crown, and it must have a crown in order to live and grow. You must strike the palm deeply through all its layers of bark to wound the crown, and a person's heart can be hurt both physically and emotionally. Eventually, both can produce fruit, but only a person can produce both physical and spiritual fruit.

A mature disciple of Jesus Christ should be producing spiritual fruit consistently. As we grow and mature in spirit, so should our spiritual fruits mature. The greatest of these fruits is love. It's not what you say, it is what you do and how you do it that ultimately matters. Love never fails. Love never gives up. Love always forgives. Love is humble and selfless. Love never dies! Let's get down to the "heart" of the matter. Everything we do and say should be from a heart of pure love. We should be in the business of healing, not wounding. If not, how are we any different from the heathen? Let love be your guide as you go through this day. Have a heart!

38. The Watchmen

"They watch over your souls…" Hebrews 13:17

Meer Kats are funny little ground hog type creatures that live on the grasslands of Africa. They live in social groups that usually consist of a matriarch, a few mature males, and lots of siblings. They all have jobs that they do. Some babysit the youngest, some dig tunnels, some scout for food, and others guard the burrow against enemies.

The watchmen stand on their hind legs, looking in every direction over and over. If they see any sign of danger, they quickly alert the others who then immediately return to defend their home.

As Christian parents, we are responsible to watch over our families. We should always be alert to what our children are doing and who they are associating with. As the priest of the family, a father should not immerse himself in so much business that he is not aware of what danger his children may be in. He will give an account before God for the souls of his children, as will the mother, who is one flesh with her spouse. There are no substitutes for involved and watchful parents. If you are a parent, determine in your heart to watch over the souls of your precious children. As much as you love them, Father God loves them much more and has put them under your charge in this world. We should take our jobs as parents seriously.

39. Chimpanzees

"Train up a child in the way he should go…" Proverbs 22:6

Each time I go to the zoo, I always visit the chimpanzees. It is fun to watch them play and swing on the ropes. I especially love the times when there happen to be mothers with their babies. Chimp mothers take their jobs very seriously. When their babies are young, they are always carried by the mothers. As they get older, they venture away from their mothers more and more to discover all the new delights of the world. Through this process moms are overseeing the discoveries. If the babies get in danger, mothers step in right away to rescue them and scold them. The moms teach the babies how to eat, climb, play safely, and give them love and protection whenever it is needed.

This is a beautiful example in nature of what God expects of parents and teachers. We must teach and train our children the right ways to go. They must be disciplined in love, not in anger, when they make wrong choices. We must love them and keep them safe. It is our task to model for them godly behavior, attitudes, and choices. If they don't see it in us, they will not form the life-long habits necessary to be overcomers in this world.

As it was said in Luke 6:40, "A student is not above his teacher, but everyone who is fully trained will be like his teacher." What will your child be like when he grows up? Look in the mirror for your answer.

40. Rainbow Promises

Isaiah 43

Rainbows are some of God's most beautiful pieces of art. They are formed by the way sunlight hits particles of water which causes certain colors of the light spectrum to be revealed. It occurs in the sky, around fountains, and next to waterfalls.

Rainbows are extra special to me. One day, I suddenly got an extreme feeling of urgency to go and sit on a rock by a rushing river and be alone with God. Days went by, and the feeling never left me. I had been praying about a very important decision in my life and seeking an answer from the Lord. Finally, my parents and I packed our bags and went to Ouray, CO. As we drove into town, we crossed a bridge over a beautiful rushing river with a big rock next to it. It was the place I had see in my spirit. That afternoon, I got my Bible, my walking stick, and a delicious chocolate shake from the homemade ice cream shop that we had passed on the way into town. I made my way to that big rock. I didn't know what to expect, but I knew that was where I was supposed to be. There, sitting on the rock, God directed me to read Isaiah 43. As I read, He put in my heart the answer I had bee asking for. I read about how God gave the rainbow to Noah as a sign of His promise to never again destroy the earth by flood. I stopped reading and looked up at the sky. Spread out gloriously over the mountain was a rainbow. It had not been there moments before. God said it was a sign that the answer He had given to me was true and would come to pass.

When I returned home later that week, I felt led to attend a church I hadn't been to before. When I sat down, I looked up at the stage. I was amazed to focus my eyes on a stained glass window on the front wall of the church. Its design was a rocky river flowing away from a mountain. At the top of the mountain was a rainbow with a cross at its base. God wanted to confirm to me that the rainbow I saw was from Him especially to me, and I did in fact receive the answer to my prayers. I was overwhelmed and humbled that God would go to such lengths just for me.

God's promises are true. We can stand on them and believe in them. If we are listening to the Holy Spirit and following His commands, He will give confirmation of His promises to us as encouragement until our faith becomes sight. Hold on to your rainbow promises! You will see your answers in due time!

41. Eating Like a Hummingbird

"…Sincere milk of the Word…" I Peter 2:2; Ephesians 5:26&27; Luke 4:4

Hummingbirds are fascinating little creatures. They are so small and delicate, yet they can fly up to 60 miles per hour. Their wings are usually moving so fast that you can almost hear them. They make an endearingly soft sound, like a hum, from which they get their name. The most surprising thing about them is their voracious appetite. They must eat one and one half to three times their weight every day. They visit hundreds of flowers in order to get enough nectar. They can starve to death in as little as one hour if they can't get food.

Many people are inclined to think they can fly about their day at 60 miles per hour, do everything well, and have energy left at the end of the day. They eat food on the go and keep on moving. Sometimes they skip meals. Eventually, this leads to illness and exhaustion.

The same is true of our spirits. We must constantly read, study and hear the Word of God so that our spirits can withstand everything we may encounter in our day. Meditate on the Word and walk in it so that you don't become sick at heart and lose faith. The enemy is always on the prowl and looking for the weak to attack. Eat! Eat! Eat! Stay strong in the Lord and in the power of His might!

42. Fog

"…After the fire, a still small voice…" I Kings 19: 11&12

Fog feels like a damp cottony cloak that has been thrown over everything. It is sometimes soft and mysteriously smoky. Other times it's thick and blindingly frightening. It can be so thick that you can't see your hand in front of your face. This kind of fog is very dangerous to move around in. You could run into something or someone else, injure yourself or others, or be attacked by something you can't see. You can be confused, lose your way, and make wrong turns. You might even get into a panic from fear of being blinded.

If you are being surrounded by a cloud of confusion and agitation, if you are lost in a myriad of complications and difficulties, the best thing to do is nothing. Satan is the author of confusion and anxiety. God does not speak or give direction in the middle of chaos. He waits for you to get quiet before Him and consciously still your mind and emotions. Then He can give you His direction and His answers. The fog of confusion will then lift, and you will be able to see the way to go clearly as the sun shines brightly on the path you are to follow once again. Listen for the still small voice. In quietness and stillness, you will find Him.

43. Valleys

"Be still and know that I am God." Psalm 6:10a; Psalm 23

    I have driven across deserts many times on my way to various mountain ranges throughout the country. It is very desolate country with only small mesquite trees, low-growing grasses, and cacti breaking up the flat landscape. It seems to stretch out forever as hour after hour goes by. Then suddenly I see a line of green off in the distance. As I get closer, the line of green begins to look like a line of bushes. A few miles closer, I can clearly see that it is a small oasis of large trees and green grasses surrounding a river. It is a lovely lush valley in the middle of the dry dusty prairie. I stop my car at the roadside pull-off next to the river. I breathe in the moist cool air coming from the direction of the water, and all the dust and weariness of the long drive is replaced with the peace of the valley. I get back in my car feeling re-energized and ready to finish the journey.

    We all go through dry desert-like experiences in our lives. We go mechanically through the motions of praise and worship and have to force ourselves to read the Bible. God seems far away and out of touch. These are the times we need to take a time out and go to our quiet place, our green river valley, and seek God's face. Be still and enter into the quiet. Breathe in the fresh wind of the Holy Spirit and soak in His presence. It's not about how you feel, it's about what you believe and know to be true. God is always with us and always ready to renew and refresh our bodies, minds, and spirits. Go to the valley. Let the Lord restore your soul.

44. Stars

"He stretched out the heavens." Job 9:8; Psalm 104:2; Isaiah 42:5; 45:12

Starlight has been a mystery and controversy for centuries. It is perhaps the strongest argument scientists have for evolution. We are told by scientists that some stars are so far away that it would be impossible for us to see their light, based upon the speed of light, unless the universe is billions of years old. Otherwise, we would see light from only a few close stars. They also tell us that the dinosaurs all died before man evolved. They base those conclusions on carbon dating and layers of the earth.

We don't have to have scientists or experiments to tell us how old the earth is or how man came to be. The Bible is the inspired, inerrant Word of God. Genesis tells us that all animal and plant life were created in the first week earth existed. It tells us that man was created in one twenty-four-hour period from the dust of the earth, and the breath of God, in His own image. It also tells us that God created the heavenly bodies and then stretched them out across the universe, in this way making it possible to immediately see light from all the stars that are now so far away. If you count the generations from Adam onward in the Old Testament, it becomes obvious that the earth can only be thousands of years old. We also know that in Noah's time, the worldwide flood covered the earth in many layers of sediment and killed all land-dwelling animals and people that were not on the ark. The pressure of the deep waters fossilized the animals and created the oil fields.

Believe God's Word. He was there when it all happened and put it in Scripture so that we would know these answers. Evolutionists want to write God out of science and creation. Who will you believe, evolutionists or your Heavenly Father and Creator, the Eye Witness?

45. The Universe Sings His Praises

"Sing unto the Lord all the earth." Psalm 96:13; Psalm 33:5

As a Christian school teacher, I have been privileged to attend conferences and hear very anointed Bible scholars teach the Scriptures. During one particular conference, I took a seminar entitled "Science and the Bible." This seminar resolved many questions I had about creation and evolution. As a child growing up in public schools, I was taught evolution, while in Sunday school, I was taught creation. I encourage everyone who lives in or is visiting north Texas to visit the Creation Evidences Museum in Glen Rose, TX. They have many Christian science resources that are invaluable to believers. These gentlemen and Christian scientists opened up to me the wonders of creation according to God's Word.

While at this conference, I learned a fascinating fact about the stars and planets. Every heavenly body emits a frequency or tone. With our modern sophisticated technology, we have recently begun to discover the truth of this. All of the planets in our solar system together make a harmonious sound. According to scientists, one tone is missing in the chord because there is a planet which was long ago destroyed and now makes the asteroid belt. So, as the Scripture says, creation literally sings to the glory of God. If the stars and planets are made to praise Him, how much more should we, His blood-bought children, sing His praises? We were made to fellowship with our Father and worship Him. We are His finest creations. We are made in His image. Let us glorify and praise our amazing Father God. Give Him the glory due His name. He is worthy of our praise!

46. Colors of Autumn

Matthew 25:14-29

Autumn is a wondrous time of year. The temperatures finally begin to cool, and the butterflies begin their southward journey. The leaves, which have all been varying shades of green, begin to slow their growth and food production, the rains come, and the change begins. Their true colors begin to come through and paint the region in luxurious Technicolor. What a magnificent sight it is!

Fall trees can teach us a wonderful truth about people. We all seem very similar while we are growing up. We go through grade school and high school. We play sports, go to church, and live with our parents or guardians. But as we get older, we begin to be more and more different from each other. We begin to select our career paths and our individuality becomes more apparent. Some start working while still in high school; others begin to prepare for college. Some go directly to work in their chosen field after graduation from high school, while others have eight or ten more years of schooling to go. We are all very different in our giftings and callings. We all show our true colors when it is our time to shine. We must take our training years seriously so that when our time of ministry comes, our true colors will not be muddied by immaturity. Don't rush into your ministry to which God has called you. He knows when it is your time to color your world.

47. Cardinals

"And the two shall become one flesh..." Ephesians 5:25-33; I Peter 34:1-22; Mark 10:8

It seems that most of the time we have at least one pair of cardinals in our back yard, sometimes two or three pairs. They are delightful to see. It is so lovely to spy the little spots of bright red amidst the evergreens and snow in the wintertime. As you may have noticed, you rarely see just one cardinal. That is because cardinals mate for life. They are always together, whether hunting for food or building nests. Cardinals are truly an example of covenant and devotion.

In a time when marriage seems to be perverted by sin and is regarded as disposable, cardinals are a reminder of what marriage was meant to be. In biblical times, covenants were very serious things. When you took an oath or covenant with someone, you were expected to give your last breath defending it.

Marriage is a covenant, brothers and sisters. It is until death do us part. There is nothing disposable about it. Yes, it involves loving each other, but on the days you aren't feeling those goose-bumps, that is when covenant comes into it. Sexual desire may fade over time. That is when real love and commitment kick in. Love and sex are not one in the same. Sex is skin deep, but real love is soul deep. The seasons in our lives change. We should be committed to grow and change together all the way to the end. This is a covenant and a privilege given to us by God to depict Jesus's love for His bride, the Church. Do not mar this picture by giving up on marriage. Show the world what real love and commitment are. Love one another as He has loved us- with an everlasting, long-suffering, and selfless love.

48. The True Vine

John 15:1-8

As a gardener, every winter I struggle with the task of cutting back my bushes and vines. It is sometimes difficult to decide how far back to prune the branches. On some plants, if you prune them too much, they will die. On others, they will get long and leggy and not flower if you cut them too long. The purpose of pruning vines is to make them bear as much fruit as possible. The unattractive and harmful growth has to be cut away for the sake of the health, beauty, and productivity of the plant.

God is pruning each one of us into His image. Those things in our lives that are not godly, He cuts off. The bad habits that make us unable to bloom, He prunes away. The process is painful and hard, but in the end, He has a beautiful and fruitful child growing strong and tall in His own image. This child will bring glory and honor to the name of Jesus Christ. Don't be afraid when God prunes you. He loves you and is doing this for your good, health, and usefulness in His kingdom.

49. The Sower

"Some fell on good soil..." Mark 4: 3-9

The spring is a time of new beginnings. Gardeners till and prepare the soil, apply fertilizer, and sow their seeds in their carefully prepared garden beds. But some accidently fall into the grass or weeds; some are blown away by the wind; still others fall on the rocks. The ones planted in the prepared beds sprout quickly and their roots grow deep into the soft ground where they get strength to become large healthy plants. The seeds that fell in the grass sprout but are quickly choked out by the spreading grass. The seeds that are blown away get heated by the harsh sun, dry up, and die. The ones which landed on the rocks are crushed by the hard surfaces and weight of the shifting rocks and never even sprout from lack of nourishment.

If we are living a spirit-filled life, we are spreading the Word of God and the love of Christ everywhere we go. Some people are ready to hear and receive it and come to the Lord readily. Others may hear it, but let someone else talk them out of believing. Some will not listen at all because they have already decided to reject the gospel of Christ. There are also people who will hear the Word and believe it, but let the troubles and trials of their lives crush their newborn faith.

It is not our responsibility to make the decision to follow Christ for others. Our part is to share the gospel with others when prompted by the Holy Spirit. Always show God's love, kindness, and forgiveness. The rest is up to that other person to choose life or death. The Holy Spirit will gently woo them and call to their spirits. Pray they will have ears to hear and that their hearts will be soft and pliable soil in which to receive the gospel of Christ and acknowledge Him as their Lord and Savior. Let the Holy Spirit do the rest.

50. The Lion of Judah

"The devil is like a roaring lion..." I Peter 5:8; Revelation 5:5

Lions are magnificent creatures. These large intimidating felines have a strong but regal bearing. They are incredible hunters and are constantly looking for the sick or weak to prey upon. They are powerful and swift in their attack. Lions are created to be skillful hunters as this is their way to be nourished and thrive.

The Bible speaks of two lions. One is compared to Satan, who looks for the spiritually weak that he will try to destroy. Satan is not an enemy to be played with. If you give him any place in your life, he will try to gain control of all of you: body, soul, and spirit. Be careful not to give him any place in your life. Don't be fooled; he is out to destroy you and separate you from God. Don't allow music, thoughts, words, or actions that are ungodly to take up residence in your mind for the devil to inhabit. Keep your mind clean and your spirit free.

The Scripture also tells us of the Lion of Judah. He is our ruler, our strong tower, and our defender. We owe our allegiance and loyalty to Him. When Satan is after us and trying to invade our thoughts or our lives, we can depend on the Lion of Judah to come to our rescue. We can call upon Him, and He will answer. He will fight for us when we have no strength.

Which pride are you in: the devourer's or the Lion of Judah's?

51. The Sand Dollar

"Suffer the little children to come unto me…" Matthew 19:13-15; Luke 9:46-48

The sand dollar is an intricate little sea creature found burrowing in the sandy shallow waters off the coastlines of the oceans in the northern hemisphere. It washes up regularly on many sea shores. It is a great object to use to tell children about the crucifixion and life of Christ. There is a star on the top which represents the star of Bethlehem. This same shape also reminds us of the rose of Sharon. It has five cuts or holes in it, representing the piercing of His head, hands, and feet. On the back of the sand dollar, you find another flower shape which resembles an Easter lily. The lily is a symbol of the resurrection of Christ. If you break the sand dollar, you will find five little pieces shaped like doves, which reminds us of how the Holy Spirit descended upon Jesus in the form of a dove at His baptism. There are many versions of the sand dollar's story, but this is obviously one of God's creations that can be used to point us directly to Jesus. Use objects and aspects of nature to help you explain the gospel of Christ to the children in your life. Jesus loves them and wants to make them His. Don't forget to minister to these little ones that are so important to the Lord.

52. Trees

"He shall be like a tree..." Psalm 1: Ephesians 3:16

When you first plant a tree, the sprout gets its nourishment from the food stored inside the seed. As it gets taller, its trunk is thin and leggy. It can be blown around and bent over by high winds, so we must tie it to a stake for support until it can stand on its own. After it is about three inches in diameter, it may not need support any longer. It then begins to grow in strength and stature year after year, bringing shade and shelter to everything smaller than itself.

Christians should grow like trees. At first, you only know how to receive teaching and training from other believers. You may have an elder Christian that you go to for support and counsel. Then you begin to stand on your own faith with the help of older and wiser Christians. As you become mature in the Word and withstand some storms and testing, you begin to be one who helps other Christians who are struggling or just beginning their walk of faith. You become a source of shelter, encouragement, and help to others who need nurturing.

Are you then able to handle everything on your own? Do mature Christians not need help and encouragement sometimes? Of course, you do! But you will first go to your roots, which are anchored and grounded in the Holy Spirit and the Word of God. Most often, you will not need other support, but when you do, give others the chance to be a blessing to you and encourage you. We are all part of the family of God and rooted into the same ground. It takes many trees to make a forest, and we are stronger when we support each other during the storms of life.

53. Fire!

"Tried by fire..." I Peter 4:12&13; James 1:12

It is so comforting on cold winter days to curl up on the couch in front of a roaring fire or build a campfire at a beautiful campsite and roast hot dogs or marshmallows. Fire is useful to cook, to provide warmth, to give light, and to purify things. Fire can also bring strength and usefulness, such as separating gold from its ore. It burns the underbrush in forests and brings new growth of wild flowers. Fire is the only thing that causes giant sequoia seeds to be released so they have a chance to germinate and become a tree.

Fire takes wood and, through a chemical reaction, changes it into ashes. Ashes have a completely different chemical composition than wood. It's impossible for ashes to turn back into wood. The molecules have been changed forever.

When trials to come into your life, remember they may have been allowed by God for many reasons. One reason is to get rid of things in your life that aren't godly, and another may be to make you strong for the Master's use. You can't be as useful to the Lord until you have allowed Him to burn away those things which hinder God's anointing in your life. Only then will you be a vessel of honor fit for His use. None of us can be perfect in this life, but the more we yield ourselves to God, the more like Jesus we can become. Surrender yourself to the fire of God, and you will come out as pure gold.

54. The Lost Sheep

"I am the good shepherd…" John 10:11; Matthew 18:12-14

I once heard a pastor preach a sermon about shepherds and their sheep that I have never forgotten. It seems that if a sheep strays away from the flock repeatedly, the shepherd will once again go and find it. Then, out of his great love and care for the sheep, take his staff and break its leg. He would lovingly bind up the broken leg and carefully place the sheep around his shoulders. He would carry the sheep, give it affection, and talk to it every day until it healed. Finally, he would unwrap the healed leg and let the sheep run free. This time, the sheep would always stay near the shepherd because he knew the shepherd's voice and knew that the shepherd cared for him.

We all have lost loved ones that we want to see saved. We are praying for them daily, but sometimes they just seem more and more lost. Don't be surprised if that loved one ends up in a terrible situation they have to suffer through. Many times God has to use hardships to get people's attention. These problems cause them to see the need for the Good Shepherd and be hungry to know the Lord. Be careful not to try to step in and fix the God-given problem of a loved one. It may be designed to bring them to salvation. Trust the Lord to work in their lives. They are His sheep and the people of His pasture. You just keep on praying and giving them to God.

55. I Come to the Garden

"Jesus went up to the hill alone to pray…" Matthew 14:23; John 6:15; Mark 6:46

Gardeners know there is always a never-ending supply of work to be done in a garden. You must fertilize, pull weeds, treat for diseases, prune, and water. In the spring and summer, I am out there one or two hours every day. No one else is home and everything is quiet. Sometimes it takes extra effort, but it must be done or the garden will die.

I have made myself a list of reasons why it is good to garden:

1) It gives oxygen back into the atmosphere.
2) It helps maintain the balance of nature and supplies wildlife with food.
3) It's good exercise for me, and I get sunshine and fresh air.
4) It helps me have balance in my mind and gives me time alone with God.

The last reason is the best one. I get so busy with my life that I don't seem to have enough time for prayer and meditation. So, I use this time to pray and meditate on God's Word. When I pray, I don't do all the talking. The Lord has a lot to say if I take the time to listen.

Whenever you have a mindless chore to do, pray and seek the Lord. He's always waiting to talk with you.

I come to the garden alone

While the dew is still on the roses,

And the voice I hear falling on my ear

The Son of God discloses.

And He walks with me and He talks with me,

And He tells me I am His own.

And the joy we share as we tarry there

None other has ever known.

By: C. Austin M

56. Sunrise

"For we wrestle not against flesh and blood…" Ephesians 6:12&18;

II Corinthians 10:3-5

Just as the sun scatters the darkness as it rises, so do the children of God bring light everywhere they go. This world is a dark and treacherous place without light. Satan, along with evil spirits, demons, strongholds, and oppression, thrive in the dark. They blind people to the truth about their lost and bound position without the salvation found in Christ Jesus.

Many of us know people who are addicted to drugs or alcohol. They are blind to their own addiction because of the darkness of their souls. Many of them are literally possessed by the demon of addiction and have no way to free themselves from its control without help. We who are the children of light must rebuke Satan and command those demons to leave in the name of Jesus, and plead the blood of Jesus over them. We must chase back the darkness and invoke the presence of the Holy Spirit when they can't do it for themselves. Only then will the light penetrate that darkness, and the Holy Spirit will be able to free them from those addictions and work in their lives.

Many Christians are intimidated by spiritual warfare, but we must take it upon ourselves to fight these battles according to the Word of God, or many will remain enslaved to addictions and demon possession forever. The devil and his forces are real, and we are charged with the pulling down of strongholds and fighting the good fight of faith. Remember, you have the power, through the name of Jesus, to bring on the sunrise in someone's life. You can bring that cleansing freeing light into a bound person's life through spiritual warfare. Our part is to pray, and stand on faith in the power of the Holy Spirit, to deliver those who are bound. There are many excellent books written about deliverance. I encourage you to read about how to help someone be free of the enemy's control. Be courageous and willing to fight for those lost souls that God loves.

57. Petrified Wood

" So I was afraid, and I went and hid your talent in the ground. See, you have what is yours." Matthew 25:14-30

The Petrified Forest National Park is full of stunning desert scenery. The most amazing things about it are the huge logs that have broken up and been scattered all around by the waters that used to flow there thousands of years ago. They were once huge trees that had grown strong, but when the waters came, the current was too strong for them, and they were uprooted by the floods and carried away. When the waters dried up, they were left stranded in the heat of the desert and gradually turned to stone.

Many Christians are like those petrified logs. They sit under great teaching service after service and gain much strength and wisdom. They grow strong in the Lord and are blessed with talent. God puts a call on their lives and gives them a mission, but they become afraid because they think they will mess up or aren't good enough or strong enough. They keep sitting there and waiting for the feeling of readiness to hit them, but it never does. They end up sitting in the pew while the rivers of living water pass through and finally dry up. Their hearts turn stony and bitter because they think God didn't want to use them and passed them by.

Saints, remember that God wants to be our strength. He never wants us to feel ready on our own. When He urges us in our spirits, we need to get out there and be obedient. Use those talents He gave you, no matter how unprepared or unworthy you may feel. Go with the living waters welling up inside you. Don't dry up and turn to stone in a pew. God needs trees planted by the rivers of living water that bring forth their fruit in season.

58. The Serpent

"The serpent spoke to Eve..." Genesis 3:1-14; I Corinthians 10:12&13;

Galatians 5:16-21

Serpents now are referred to as snakes. They are very quiet animals. They move slowly and deliberately and seem harmless, but after they have been allowed to sneak up on their prey, they will suddenly strike their victims a fatal blow. They will then inject a poison into the defenseless animals that will kill them within minutes. The snakes will then swallow them whole.

The devil is ruthless. He is an attractive foe. He makes himself appear to be friendly and enticing at first. He makes his plans sound really great. We begin to believe his lies and go along with him. We get more and more involved in the sin, until suddenly we are trapped. Sin always looks good to us. If it didn't we wouldn't want to sin. The devil's name is Lucifer. He was given that name before being cast out of heaven. Lucifer means light. He was beautiful! He can still look very appealing when he wants to.

Beware of the enticements of the enemy. At the first sign of temptation, we should run from it. Don't entertain it for even a minute. If he gains your mind, he can draw you in and attack you. Keep your thoughts on God, set your affections on things above, and you will be hidden under the blood of Christ in God and protected from the enemy of your soul.

59. Diamonds

"When he is tried..." James 1:12; I Peter 1:7

Diamonds are the most precious and beautiful of all gems, but diamonds start out as common pieces of carbon. They have layer upon layer of soil and rock covering them over time. They get buried deep into the earth and are pressed and heated many times before they become diamonds. When a diamond is finally formed, it is still sometimes misshapen and covered with other rocks and dirt. It has to be found, mined from the earth, and cleaned of all dirty surface material. Then it is examined by experts to locate its flaws and to determine how it can be cut to produce the most beautiful and shiny gemstone possible.

We are God's diamonds. We are pressured and heated by trials many times during our lives. Along the way, our sins and secrets are uncovered and washed by the blood of Jesus. We are cut, ground, and polished by the many lessons the Holy Spirit teaches us. We are made into a gem that perfectly fits our assigned space in the crown of Christ and used for His glory. There, the radiance and beauty of the diamond of your life can reflect the image of Jesus Christ and shine for all those around you to be blessed by. Stand up under the pressure, withstand the heat, and you will be radiant in due time.

60. Roots

"Let all bitterness, wrath, and anger..." Hebrews 12:15; Romans 11:16;

Ephesians 4:30-32

Every year, I am reminded of deep roots. In the early spring, I have to go into my garden and pull up all the weeds that have encroached into my flower beds, but there are some kinds whose roots have gone deep and require a big shovel to get out of the ground. It's hard work to get them out, but if I leave the tap root in, the weed will grow right back.

Bitterness, hate, and unforgiveness are the weeds in our spirits that have long tap roots. If we hold on to unforgiveness and let it grow in our hearts, it can turn into bitterness. Bitterness has the power to not only make our spirits sick, but it can also make us physically sick. We should always ask God to help us pull out feelings of hurt and unforgiveness when they are fresh. They have not had the chance to take root in our souls and damage our minds and bodies. He will help us to forgive. We don't have to feel like it, we just have to take a step and begin to change. Stop dwelling on the hurt. Then forgiveness can finally take root in our hearts and bring healing. Our spirits will finally be able to receive the blessings of God again in the clean fertile soil of our hearts. Our bodies can begin to heal through the fresh life-giving flow of Living Water that begins as a result of choosing to forgive. If not, we will be slowly consumed and destroyed by our bitterness. Choose to be free from the roots of bitterness from the past, and move on to renewal of body, soul, mind, and spirit.

61. Parenthood

"Whom the Lord loves, He chastens…" Hebrews 12:5-11

It was fascinating watching the mountain big horn sheep doing a balancing act on the side of Checkerboard Mountain in Zion National Park. In spite of the steepness, when her baby got tired this momma shaded her baby while the daddy waited patiently ahead. These parents are doing the right thing in sheltering their baby in a dangerous place.

Children today are growing up in a society which has virtually destroyed biblical parenthood. As an educator for more than thirty years, I have had a front row seat to witness the changes in American children. When prayer was removed from our public schools, we spiritually tied God's hands from the rearing of our children. There has been less and less discipline over the years, so that now children are practically raising themselves. More and more children are fatherless and are being taught values by television, movies, and music. If a parent spanks a child, our society sees it as abuse and tries to take the child away from that parent.

All this lack of proper discipline is creating generations of children with little self-control, no respect for adults, and a self-centered point of view. The real truth is that if a child has no limits, he is unhappy and insecure. If he is not disciplined, he doesn't feel loved or cared about. If he is given too much, he never appreciates anything.

Godly parents, obey what the Bible teaches and discipline your children. Lovingly paddle them when necessary; scold them when they're selfish; make them earn special things instead of just giving them what they want. Give them chores at home to develop responsibility and pride in a job well done. Have them answer you with "yes, sir" and "yes, ma'am," and don't allow them to argue with you. God chastens us because He loves us. He doesn't leave us to raise ourselves. He disciplines us because He has our good in mind. Love your children like God loves you. Don't allow your children to feel like orphans with no one to be accountable to. Hold up a godly standard for them to follow. They are our future leaders. What do you want the world to look like forty years from now?

62. Mature Fruit

"Honor your father and your mother..." Ephesians 6:1-3; I Peter 5:5

Notice that it takes several years before fruit trees are able to bear fruit. Also, notice that if you pick the fruit before it is ripe, it is sour, hard, or tasteless. Only when fruit has fully ripened on the tree does it possess all of the vitamins, nutrients, and antioxidants that it is meant to have. When you eat a piece of ripe fruit, it is juicy, delicious, sweet, and very nutritious.

Today's world looks down on the elderly and thinks of them as an inconvenience. They're to be made to retire as quickly as possible and put in retirement centers where they eventually become sick and die. The young people think their elders don't understand what they face in their lives and see them as old-fashioned. The old ones don't have any importance to them.

The Bible says we're to respect and look up to the elderly. They've gone through much in their lives and can provide invaluable wisdom and advice. They have mature fruit to offer to their friends and families if given a chance. There are really no new trials or problems under the sun. They're just wrapped in different paper of today's world. Reach out to those parents, grandparents, aunts, and uncles in your life. There's much spiritual nutrition to be had if we take the time to listen. Honor the elderly and receive from them. Much treasure lies there for the taking, if we take the time to listen.

63. Disk Flowers

"We are the body of Christ..." Ephesians 4:11-16

When you look at a disk flower, how many flowers do you see? Most would answer one. In actual fact, one disk flower really contains tens to hundreds of tiny flowers in its center. Butterflies and bees come from far and wide to eat their nectar. Together, those tiny flowers can feed many insects, but if those tiny flowers were on their own, insects would have great difficulty finding them and go hungry, perhaps even die.

Churches, whether in homes or traditional church buildings, are like disk flowers. When the body of Christ comes together to fellowship, worship, and hear the Word of God taught, it is like a disk flower in full bloom and will attract many people. Hungry people who need a touch from God will come from miles away because they smell the fragrance of the worship being sent up by God's people. They'll be hungry for God's Word and be able to feast on the Bread of Life that is being shared. Church, come together in Jesus name, and let the body of Christ feed a hungry world.

64. Sand

"He gives me beauty for ashes..." Isaiah 61:3; Romans 8:28; Job 5:7

I recently learned an amazing thing about sand. If there's a violent electrical rainstorm, lightening will sometimes strike an object on a beach. If that lightening current is conducted into the sand, thousands of degrees of heat will come into contact with the sand and all the sand particles around it forming a beautiful free-form glass sculpture. There are stores in many beach communities that sell these sculptures or have them on display. They're works of nature's power and electrical explosions that have turned ordinary sand into beautiful objects of art.

Bad things happen in life. They happen to all of us. Whether it is the loss of a loved one, a broken relationship, unfair treatment, a trial, or the loss of a job, we all experience them. But not everyone allows God to bring about good in their lives from it. We need to trust God that everything that comes our way that feels bad to us God can use for His glory. He can and does work all things together for our good. It may not happen immediately. You may have to wait for it, but our God is a good and faithful Father. He never makes us suffer without reward or wisdom following. He always gives us beauty for ashes, the oil of joy for mourning, and the garment of praise for the spirit of heaviness. God can and will turn your sand into a beautiful glass sculpture if you will only trust Him!

65. Weeds

"...Entertain angels unaware..." Hebrews 13:1-3; I Kings 17:9-16

What are weeds? One person's weed is another person's prized plant. There's an old saying, "Beauty is in the eye of the beholder." We have many plants in our butterfly garden that a lot of people would call weeds, but they're food or host plants which butterflies use and can't live without.

I may be going along with my regularly scheduled life and suddenly a complication pops up. I get frustrated at this interruption and complain to myself about this inconvenience. I think about the time I've lost and wonder how I'm going to make up for this weed that has suddenly come up in my garden of life. That weed may be your spouse getting a flat tire, your babysitter not showing up, or a family member getting sick. If you are praying over your day each morning and walking in obedience to the Lord, He will sometimes give you detours to take along your daily path. These "weeds" may look like a problem to you, but to God it may be an opportunity, a chance to be a blessing to someone else. That nuisance may make someone else's day, and we may never know it. It may also have delayed you just enough to keep you out of a car accident or grave danger. Praise God and thank Him for the weeds!

66. Rhinoceros

"Put on the whole armor of God..." Ephesians 6:11-18

A rhinoceros is a common sight in zoos around the country. They're one of God's strangest creatures. They have thick plates of tough hide and fat which cover the entire body, except it's stomach and underarms. It's very difficult to penetrate the tough hide. It's the protection God has given these astonishing creatures to keep them from harm and injury.

As children of God, we're told to put on the whole armor of God every day. We're constantly fighting a battle with Satan and all his forces for our immortal souls. All these pieces of armor are for the front of our bodies. This is because we're to stand up to him and attack Satan head on! Soldiers can't defeat enemies if they're running away from them. We're to quench the fiery darts of the wicked with the shield of faith. We're not to turn our backs and get burned.

The armor of God is something you can put on every day as you get dressed in the morning. Leaving home without it is like going out naked. It is very important to put it on every day without fail. Don't be left unprotected from your enemies!

67. Morning Dew

"Early will I seek You." Proverbs 8:17; I Thessalonians 5:17; Psalm 63:1

Early in the mornings, when the first rays of the dawning sun creep across the sky, the ground begins to glisten from the early refreshment of the morning dew. All the flora, and even the birds, are cooled and quenched by this first-light blessing of life-giving water. Now they can face the day with renewed energy and nourishment.

We, too, need a fresh drink of Living Water as we start the day. Our first words upon awakening should be, "Good morning, Lord. Thank you for another day of life. How can I serve you today?"

Without a fresh anointing of the Holy Spirit and His guidance, we can very well miss blessings and opportunities that come our way in this new day. We're all busy and have a lot on our minds, but we can always pray anywhere and anytime.

Keep yourself attuned to that still small voice as you go about your day. Make sure not to miss out on God's special appointments. There are blessings awaiting us in every new day.

68. Fragrance

"...Burned incense on the altar..." Romans 8:3&4; Luke 7:44-48

There are countless smells in the world being emitted by all kinds of plants, animals, and other things. It amazes me that many different kinds of flowers have their own distinctly beautiful fragrance, and some smell equally terrible. God obviously thinks that having a smell is important. Isn't that curious?

In the Bible, we read that in the temple, incense was constantly burning on the altar. We know that the wise men brought frankincense to baby Jesus and that Mary Magdalene bathed Jesus' feet with costly perfume. In the Old Testament, praise is likened to fragrant oil going down Aaron's beard. So, fragrance is symbolic of the praises of God's people, continually rising up before the throne of God. Our praise is a sweet incense to Him. God breathes in our worship and praise, and it makes His heart glad. The Lord delights in our worship, and He comes and inhabits, or lives in, the praises of His people. This is also of great benefit to the worshipper. It helps us to enter into God's presence and put ourselves into a position to receive God's Word for our lives and situations. It releases the power of God to come and work on your behalf. Do you need to hear from God? Begin sending up the fragrance of praise and worship before the altar of God. Open up your heart and receive God's presence. He will come and fill you and overtake your obstacles and bring victories in your battles as He fills your life with His loving presence.

69. Timing

"To everything there is a season..." Ecclesiastes 3:1-8; II Corinthians 1:20;

Hebrews 6:10-15

In autumn, seeds fall everywhere. They will not be able to grow or even sprout if they fall into the wrong place. If they're fooled into sprouting too early, they could die or be severely damaged by a late freeze. Some seeds may be kept in storage for years until the gardener finds the perfect place and time for them to grow and bloom. Some seeds may naturally fall into good places, but may lie just under the ground waiting for several years for the right amount of sunlight temperatures, and water to make it germinate.

Never give up on dreams that God puts in your heart. His timing is perfect. He doesn't operate on the same plane of time as we do. Don't think He has forgotten what you have asked Him for. He never forgets. Perhaps the answer has just not had enough time to come to light. You may not be ready to receive the answer yet. Keep trusting God and thanking Him for the fulfillment of that dream. If it's His will, it'll happen at the appointed time. God is never late, nor is He slack in carrying out His promises to you. The answer is on its way!

70. The Golden Hour

"Where any two of you agree..." Matthew 18:18-20; Acts 2:46&47

The golden hour is that special time when the sun is low in the sky and everything is gloriously bathed in a golden light. The day's work is over and it is time for family and rest. These are the hours we look forward to. They're those precious few hours we can sometimes call our own.

It is so important to keep communication and closeness in your family, the few evening hours that you have with family are like golden treasures. Make a point of having your family sit down together for a home-cooked meal at least once a week. Afterwards, have a family activity, and then end the night with a song, scripture or devotion, and prayer. Strive to keep your family spiritually together. It is vital to your relationships with each other and God. They'll experience God's presence in the most intimate setting possible. It is here at home that they'll best learn to sincerely pray and worship the Lord. Pray over each one's needs as a family, and help your young ones to gain confidence to lead the family in prayers. In this way, faith in God will become real and relevant to their lives as they see family prayers answered. Be a faith-building family! Make family night and home church regular weekly activities.

71. Air

"Seek first the kingdom of God…" Matthew 6:33

"Be filled with the Holy Spirit…" Ephesians 5:17&18

We must breathe in air constantly or we will suffocate and die. Our physical bodies cannot survive without the breath of life-giving air.

Spiritually, we need the fresh wind of the Holy Spirit to breathe life into us every moment of every day. We must constantly be filled with the Holy Ghost and be led by the Spirit or we can, at any moment, lose the blessing of God on our lives. Without that fresh anointing each day, you can become spiritually sick and lacking in the life of God flowing through your mind and heart. This will leave you spiritually defenseless and in danger of making bad decisions or saying inappropriate things. The consequences of being out of the will of God for even one minute can be catastrophic to God's plan for your life. Always seek God's will and constant presence first in your life and all the other things you need will be taken care of. God comes first! His presence is more necessary than air.

72. Variety

"He knit you together in your mother's womb..." Psalm 139:1-18; Matthew 25:14-29

There's great variety in nature; we have animals, plants, and people. In those groups, we have countless subspecies, all with their own special looks, strengths, weaknesses, and characteristics. God loves variety. If it weren't for a variety, we'd have a very boring existence. The ecosystems would not work without diversity. Many jobs would be left undone, and life would cease to exist. Variation is a necessity.

The next time you find yourself wishing you could be like someone else, or thinking that you aren't important or needed, remember that God made you for a special purpose. Your life is important in God's plan. He gave to you at least one special talent. You aren't meant to be like anyone else. You should develop your talent to its best and highest level. Celebrate your individuality! God does. Allow Him to use you for the purpose for which you were created. Be yourself and rejoice in who you are. There's no one else like you in the whole world. There never has been, nor ever will be, another you!!

73. Roses

"Beauty is fleeting..." Proverbs 31:30; I Samuel 16:7

Roses are arguably the most beautiful flowers God has created. Not only are they lovely to look at, coming in almost every color of the rainbow, but they have a variety of delicious scents, too. But in contrast, most roses also have very sharp thorns on their stems.

There's a symbolic deeper lesson to be learned from the rose. People are often blessed with great outward beauty. As a culture and a society, we put great emphasis and importance on outward beauty. Many men want physically perfect women and cast aside those who don't fit that mold. Lots of women want strong and handsome men and discount men who don't measure up to their standards. Many times, as they get to know that raving beauty or hunk, thorns and weaknesses in their character begin to come to light. It becomes apparent that they've been trading on their good looks instead of developing their character and maturing in their walk with God. They suddenly seem far less attractive than they first appeared to be.

Remember that outward beauty fades over time. The beauty that counts is the inward beauty. The plainest of people can become the loveliest when you get to know them. Remember that God looks on the heart. That is what truly matters. The garments of righteousness and holiness make everyone beautiful in their own way.

When a rose petal is crushed, it releases more of its lovely fragrance. What scent comes from you when you are crushed?

74. The Fragrance After the Rain

"The trying of your faith works patience…" James 1:2-4; I Corinthians 10:13

One of my favorite smells in the world is the smell of rain-washed earth and air. Rain does so many wonderful things. It cleanses the air of its contaminants and softens the soil so the roots of plants can grow deeper and stronger. Rain brings fresh water so that the lives of plants and animals are sustained, and they can grow to maturity. The sound of rain is a soothing lullaby that can help us fall asleep, but the smell of rain is also invigorating and reminds me of the renewal of life.

Someone once said, "In every life, a little rain must fall." What is closer to the truth is that a lot of rain falls in most of our lives. Sometimes we are flooded. We tend to look at those showers of trials as bad things that bring problems to us. When in actual fact, they are showers of blessings. Look at those showers as tools that bring health, growth, and strength to us, and cleanse us of things that are contaminating our spirits, minds, and bodies. Without this spiritual rain, we would die. After the storms have passed, we will offer up the sweet-smelling fragrance of praise to our God for His blessing of rain on our lives. We may not enjoy the storms when they pass over us, but we can look forward to the blessings and spiritual gifts that come as a result. Thank God for rain!

75. The Lamb of God

"Behold the Lamb of God..." John 1:29, 3:14-18: Ephesians 2:4-10

Little lambs are so cute when they're first born. They're all legs and wobbly on their feet. Some lambs are all white with wool like snow. They're perfect, spotless, and innocent little ones.

In the Old Testament, it was the regular practice of the Jews to bring a perfect lamb to the temple for sacrifice to cover the sins of their family with its shed blood. They did this because the temple priests had taught them that this was the law of God, but they didn't understand why they had to do this. What was the reason for this? What did it mean?

It was, of course, the foreshadowing of the Lamb of God, Jesus Christ, who would come to earth to be the sacrifice for the sins of all mankind. All our sins- past, present, and future, are washed by the shed blood of Christ. He paid the price for sin, which is death, so that we who call on His name would not have to die for our sins. Oh, what freedom we have in Christ! By grace we're saved through faith, not of works, because then man would think he could earn his own salvation. When we receive Christ, we become new creatures. Our sinful nature is no longer in charge, and we're free to choose not to sin. If we do sin, it isn't fun like it used to be. We instantly feel guilt or regret because the holiness of the Holy Spirit is now residing inside us. Then, we plead the blood of Jesus over that sin and continue to walk in our salvation. If we needed to be saved over again every time we sin, Christ would have had to die over and over again. Because Jesus died for all the sin of all time, we're no longer slaves to sin. Thank God! Don't let occasional sin get you down. Just give it to God and go on, but don't use that grace as an excuse to sin and grieve the Holy Spirit. We're walking in God's merciful grace. Remember, you didn't earn your salvation, Jesus did.

76. Sharks

"Judge not, lest you be judged." Matthew 7:1-5; John 8:7

I have seen many documentaries about sharks They are constantly moving and have voracious appetites. They are known to even eat their young and each other. They can smell blood in the water miles away, and they go into a feeding frenzy when prey is found.

Unfortunately, there are those in the Church that act just like sharks. They sit in judgment over others. They destroy baby Christians by jumping on them about their mess-ups. They are on constant alert for any gossip they can spread about others, and they are the first ones to stop fellowshipping with someone who is in trouble. The terrible fact is that the Church often destroys its young, weak, and wounded instead of helping, encouraging, and forgiving them. Did Jesus ostracize, convict, or punish Mary Magdalene for her sins? Did He chase away the lepers because they were sick or chain up the demon possessed? No! He helped them, healed them, and forgave them. Most importantly, He loved them unconditionally. Church, it is not our job to judge others or spread gossip about them. Be careful about your judgments. Only God is our judge. The Scripture says that if we judge, we will be judged. If you are without sin, you can cast the first stone at a sinner, but no one is without sin. Only Jesus was without sin, and even He refused to cast the first stone. Love one another as Christ has loved you! Forgive and encourage; refuse to spread rumors. Church, let's be love and light to all around us, both saved and unsaved. Love will cover a multitude of sins.

77. The New Earth

"There will be a new Heaven and a new Earth…" Isaiah 65:17&18;

Revelation 21:1-7

When Jesus Christ returns to Earth, He will set up His kingdom, and it shall be without end. The Word of God makes many references to a new Heaven and a new Earth. If you were to read all the references to these two phrases, you would discover something exciting and miraculous. God promises that He will recreate the earth the way it was before sin entered the picture. The heavens will be made new as well. The new earth and the new Jerusalem will be united. Heaven will come down and become part of the new Earth. We were designed to live on Earth, and we are joint heirs with Christ. We will live and reign on the new Earth with Christ forever. That means that everything that was destroyed or became extinct could be found on the new Earth. It will be recreated in its most perfect state for God's children to enjoy. Only those things which bring glory to God will be allowed in the new creation. The devil and all who followed him will be cast into the lake of fire and suffer eternal punishment. He will never be allowed to torment God's people ever again. Praise the Lord for our incredible inheritance through Christ Jesus!

78. Heaven

"No eye has seen nor ear heard the things which God has prepared..."

II Corinthians 2:9; John 14:1-3; Revelations 21:9 & 22:5

Sometimes when we see a stream tumbling through a forest, the sun setting over the ocean, snow-capped mountains, or a field of rainbow-colored wild flowers, we think to ourselves, "This is just like heaven." The most beautiful breath-taking sights in the world can't compare to the magnificent beauty of heaven.

When the Bible was written, there wasn't much of a chance for eyewitnesses to see heaven because if their hearts stopped beating, there were no machines or doctors able to bring them back to life. With our current technology, that now happens every day. It's a fact that at the moment we die, our spirit simply snaps out of our bodies, and we're free to rise up and out of them. We see and hear everything going on at that time. Many doctors have written books about what their patients told them upon returning to life after being clinically dead. Some saw heaven, and some saw hell. Many accounts are true, and some are made up. The fact remains that heaven is real, and God has prepared a place for all believers. That place is far beyond anything we can possibly imagine. People have reported that in heaven, the colors have more than one dimension, and everything makes a glorious sound. Together, they make a beautiful symphony of praise to God. There are gorgeous, flowers, trees, mountains, forests, plants, and animals. It is a place where people fellowship, work in meaningful pursuits, and commune with God. The city has transparent golden streets and buildings made of precious stones. A beautiful crystal-clear river runs through it where the water of life flows. Beside the river, the trees of life grow. They bare twelve fruits, a different one each month, for food.

If you believe on the name of the Lord Jesus Christ as your Savior, this place was built for you! Thank you, Heavenly Father, for a future of eternal life. Thank you for the precious gift of salvation through the shed blood of Jesus Christ! Because of Jesus, I have everlasting life in paradise to look forward to. Praise the Lord!

79. Ashes

"Ashes to ashes..." Ecclesiastes 12:7; "For I know the plans I have..."

Jeremiah 29:11

It is always difficult for us when we lose people we love, especially those who are closest to us. If that person was not saved, it is truly a tragedy and very hard to deal with, but that person made the choice not to except Christ. There's nothing more we can do for them. We should instead concentrate on those around us who are still here and can still be saved. This is our mission while we're here on Earth. The only things we can take with us to Heaven are other people. We need to take with us as many as we can.

If the person you lost is a believer in Christ, then you should be focusing not on your own loss, but what they've gained. What a joyous time for them! No more suffering or pain; only joy and glorious life everlasting. In a sense, you aren't grieving for that person who has passed on, you are really grieving for yourself and how much you miss them. Set your mind and heart on the eternity that you will be spending with them in Heaven and on the new Earth. Let your grief become joy and your crying become singing. God has a wonderful future planned for His children. You have a future and a hope!

80. The Harvest

"The fields are white unto harvest..." John 4:35-38; Luke 10:2;

"I am not ashamed of the Gospel..." Romans 1:16

It is always a satisfying experience to me when I get to pick the ripe fruits and vegetables from my garden. I have tilled and amended the ground, planted my seeds, pulled out the weeds, watered, fertilized, treated for diseases, and now, finally, I get to reap my harvest. A lot of hard work has gone into it, and I have the honor of feeding my family and friends fresh, organic home-grown food that is a gift of my time and work to them.

Growing food is such a great life lesson! When we're saved, God intends us to be witnesses to the lost people around us and sometimes in other parts of the world. If we weren't meant to do this, then God would just bring us on up to Heaven the moment we were saved. There would be no point to let us endure the trials and sufferings of this world. It is our responsibility to work together to bring in the harvest of souls in the name of Jesus Christ. Some of us will water, some will pull out the weeds, some will fertilize the Word that has already been planted in hearts, and others will reap the harvest when people are ready to be saved. Let's all do our jobs to bring in the harvest!

The world is going to hell if we don't tell them about Jesus. We can't let the media, the government, the president, or anyone else tell us that Christianity is bad or outdated. We can't be ashamed to spread the gospel of Christ. Jesus is coming back soon! The signs are all around us, and time is running out. When the Holy Spirit nudges you to speak for Him, open your mouth and He will fill it and give you the boldness to speak for Him.

Pray for all those who are faithful to the end and are being brutally executed for their faith. Pray that God will take them the instant before their execution. The Bible says we will not see death, and I truly believe that. Pray that many will come to Christ because of their powerful witness to the end. They'll receive martyr's crowns and great rewards in Heaven. Church, quickly bring in the harvest. Jesus is coming soon! Even so, come Lord Jesus!

81. Interdependency

"And the whole body, being fitly joined together..." I Corinthians 12:4-31

In nature, there are many chains of dependency: food chains, the water cycle, and ecosystems. In particular, plants and animals are especially dependent on each other for survival. Through photosynthesis, plants breathe in carbon dioxide, and expel oxygen, while people and animals breathe in oxygen and expel carbon dioxide. It is impossible for plants and animals to survive without each other.

The body of Christ has many different parts. Just as in nature, all things depend on each other, so does the proper working of the Church. There must be prophets and teachers in order for the Church to be properly instructed. There must be those who give words of wisdom and knowledge for guidance, encouragement, and confirmation. The body of Christ needs prayer warriors who spend many hours on their faces before God. Evangelists must reach the lost with the Gospel of Christ. Pastors are needed to support the members of the body. Deacons and elders serve the Church in matters of counsel and business. Givers are used to supply the needs of the body of Christ and provide funds for missionary endeavors. The Church needs those who have the gift of faith and the gift of healing to minister to those who are going through trials or are sick. There are many others as well, but everyone is necessary to the healthy function of the body of Christ. Be sure to do your part by developing and using the gifts that God has placed within you. Step out in faith, and God will do the rest.

82. Moonlight

"Let your light so shine…" Matthew 5:14-16

"Everyone practicing evil hates the light…" John 3:19-21

As we all learned in elementary school, the moon does not give off light of its own. It shows a reflection of the sun's light, like a mirror. It isn't as noticeable in the daytime, but when it's dark, we see bright moonlight.

Believers are like moons. We reflect the Son's light that is within us through the Holy Spirit. When things are going well, it is easy for the light to shine, so it's not so obvious to those around us in hours of happiness and ease. It is when hard times come and things look really dark in our lives that our moonlight shines brightly to those who are watching how we deal with adversity. If we go through trials with unwavering faith and peace, our witness for the Lord shines out to those who are in darkness. Let your moon reflect the presence of God, especially in your darkest hours. The difference in how Christians respond to trials is what gets the attention of a lost world. Our confidence in God and His ability to get us through triumphantly speaks volumes to those around us. Determine to show His love and faithfulness in your life by exhibiting praise, joy and faith through your trying times, and let others see that there is still hope for them, too.

83. Songbirds

"Singing to yourselves with psalms, hymns, and spiritual songs…"

Ephesians 5:19&20; Psalm 32:7

Have you noticed how intricately music has been woven into creation? Even stars and planets emit harmonious frequencies. Animals make calls to one another with a series of tones or single notes. Birds most especially have the ability of making beautiful music with their varied notes and calls. The wind, also, can whistle through the trees and grasses making its own songs.

People have a very unique gift of song that the rest of creation does not have. We can sing an infinite number of songs using a myriad of note combinations. We were made to sing songs of praise in worship to our great Creator God. The Bible instructs us to always have a song in our hearts. Singing is not only uplifting, but it's also a form of warfare that can quickly defeat Satan's attacks on our minds. It has also been proven to clear out sinuses and strengthen vocal chords, bringing physical healing. It is great medicine when depression is trying to overtake you. Whether singing as a group or by ourselves, it should be a part of our spiritual daily walk with the Lord. Don't forget your daily dose of music today!

84. Mimicry

"It is better to be hot or cold..." Revelation 3:15&16

In the insect world, there are several insects that mimic another insect. They were created this way because they are afforded protection from enemies who are fooled into thinking that they are the more harmful insect that they resemble. A queen butterfly mimics the poisonous, bad-tasting monarch. A syrphid fly looks just like a bee, but really has no stinger.

Mimicry is a good thing in nature, but not in people. There are people who go to church and try to talk and act like they are Christians, but in reality, they are not truly saved because they have never prayed the prayer of salvation or made Jesus Lord of their lives. Their prayers are empty and their good works will be of no effect. God hates hypocrites. No one can be good enough to work their way into Heaven. We are only saved by the blood of Christ and the forgiveness of our sins. We cannot serve God and the flesh. You are either a born-again Christian, or you are not. There is no middle ground. Choose Christ and live, or you have refused Him and will die.

85. The River of Life

"...I will guide you with my eye..." Psalm 32: 8-10

This is the famous "Horseshoe Bend" in the Grand Canyon. It is awe-inspiring when looking down on it from a very precipitous drop-off far above. From the top, you can see the big three-quarter circle the river makes, before going off in a new direction. The canyon is very deep and the boats look like ants by the shore.

In the course of our life's journey, we start out thinking that we know exactly where our ship will sail; we have every stop planned, how long we will sail, and in what direction. But as we sail along, we seem to be continually turning and not stopping where we planned. All the scenery keeps looking the same, and we feel like we are just going in circles with no straight smooth sailing in sight. Our plan seems ruined.

We must remember that God sits on high and sees the big picture. If we are allowing Him to guide us with His eye, we will never wreck or make a wrong turn. He knows what is best and will keep us on the right path. Let Him be your pilot!

86. Spiritual Food

"Desire the sincere milk of the Word..." I Peter 2:2-5; I John 4:1-3

When I was teaching elementary school, we always discussed proper nutrition. The easiest way to teach it was to tell my students to eat a rainbow every day. Meats, vegetables, fruits, grains, fats, and dairy are crucial to a balanced healthy diet. The colors of fruit and vegetables are indicative of the nutrients they possess. If your plate looks like a rainbow of colors, then you have a well-balanced meal. Your body will thrive and have what it needs for optimum functionality.

As you read, listen to, and study God's Word, be sure to have a balance. Don't just read your favorite passages every day. Read from different parts of the Bible. Make a point of reading a book in God's Word that you know little about. Some passages are harder to understand and sometimes are not easy to hear, but they are necessary to make us spiritually balanced, healthy, and strong in the Lord. If you don't understand something, there are many Spirit-led commentaries and concordances that are available on-line and in book stores. Don't just drink the milk, eat some of the meat, too!

Listen to many different pastors and teachers. Read lots of Christian books. Get a balanced view of God's Word. Remember to test the spirits and see if your spirit bears witness with the teachings. Make the Holy Spirit your master teacher. Men are imperfect, but God's Word is all truth. Be open to personal instruction from the Holy Spirit as He guides you into all truth and as you feast on the Bread of Life.

87. Organic Food

"…Added to the church daily…" Acts 2:41-47

The Bible makes many references to fruit, bread, milk, meat, corn, wine, and water. Food is obviously very important to every living organism. As I wrote about in the previous devotion, we should be sure not to eat anything chemically treated or genetically modified. The best way to get good nutrition is to eat only organic foods. These foods have the highest possible nutritional value available and are most easily digested. They are 100% recognizable as food to your digestive system and will not be so easily stored as fat, which is what happens to highly processed foods your system doesn't recognize. Purified water and spring water are the best to drink and bathe in. Grow your own organic garden so that you and your family can have delicious vine-ripe vegetables to provide the maximum nutrients. As a bonus, gardening gives you vitamin D from the sunshine and healthful exercise.

So, where can I get fed the richest spiritual food and get the most authentic ministry and real encouragement? The answer may surprise you. The first churches were not in large halls or arenas where thousands of people gathered, but in the homes of believers. People need personal contact and relationships in order to receive true ministry. Large church service productions are entertaining and exciting, but tend to be impersonal and not conducive to developing relationships. I have many friends who have been faithful church members for years and have become disillusioned by the traditional church because they were not receiving personal ministry, and it was all about money. These same dear people did not fall away from God, but went on to follow God in a personal way or became part of home fellowships- the organic grass roots of our faith.   In this atmosphere of intimacy, people truly relax, relate, and receive encouragement and healing when they need it most. Personal ministry is vital to a healthy church. Since so many Christians have realized the importance of relevant personal ministry, many home churches have sprung up around the world and are seeing thousands of people accepting Christ in these intimate places of worship. For this reason, large churches also need to have small home fellowship groups where personal ministry may take place. Traditional churches are blessings to many, but many others prefer a more personal ministry. We all need to go back to the organic way of having church. Spread God's Word from person to person and house to house. Make your home a place where real ministry thrives through personal relationships and true fellowship with other believers.

88. Geodes

"He uses the foolish to confound the wise..." I Corinthians 1:25-29; I Samuel 16; Matthew 21:16

Geodes are quite interesting. They are ordinary ugly brown, gray, or white rocks on the outside. You wouldn't give them a second look because they appear worthless. But if you break them open, you will find a hollow cavity lined with beautifully colored crystals or gems. Many beautiful rock displays and jewelry are created from them.

It has been said, "Never judge a book by its cover." That is never more accurate than when applied to people. Many people are overlooked for important work or ministry because of their appearance. They might be too short, too skinny, too ugly, or too fat in others' eyes, but we should follow God's anointing and leading in a person's life, not what we find physically appealing.

In the Old Testament, is the story of David and how he was chosen to be king. His father paraded all of his older brothers before the prophet. He thought they were the most qualified to be King of Israel. After all of them had been presented, the prophet asked if he had any more sons. Well, only the little one who was out herding the sheep was left. The father didn't consider him qualified because he was young and inexperienced, but God saw his heart and his inward potential. He knew David would be a man after His own heart.

Never judge others by their outward appearance. If God directs you to someone for a special assignment, follow what God says, even if the person doesn't seem the right one to you. There may be hidden treasure inside that geode that only Gods sees. Everyone deserves the chance to become the man or woman God intends them to be. Trust God's leading. He knows what's best for everyone. When the heart's treasure is revealed everyone will benefit from its beauty.

89. Cultivation

"Break up the fallow ground..." Jeremiah 4:3; Psalm 139:23&24; Ezekiel 11:19-20

When I am beginning a new garden space, I first till the ground. It is full of weeds, roots, and sometimes rocks. The heavy clay soil is in hard hunks and isn't suitable for growing a successful garden. I pull out all the bad stuff and add a little water to soften the clods of dirt. Then I till it again. At that point, I add compost, organic fertilizer, and sand, then mix it all up with the tiller. Finally, I smooth it out to level making it ready to receive the new seeds and plants. It's a hard job and requires a lot of work, but I'm rewarded with a beautiful healthy garden.

There have been times in my life when I felt that I couldn't hear from God. I couldn't feel His presence and seemed to be stuck out in the middle of a spiritual desert all alone. What was going on? Had God deserted me when I needed Him? No, of course not. I had allowed some things in my life to come between God and me. It had built up some hard places in my heart that were keeping me from continuing to grow in God. After a while, I began to realize that since God is perfect, I had to have something wrong with me. I asked the Lord to show me the fallow ground in my spirit that was causing me to be separated from His presence. I repented of those things that were revealed to me and asked God to replace my fallow heart with a pliable heart of flesh. He did. I slowly began to sense God's presence more and hear His voice again as I had before. Check the garden of your heart regularly for weeds, rocks, and roots. Don't allow them to create fallow ground in your heart that cannot be cultivated by the Holy Spirit. Keep a soft, pure, and tender heart before God so He can grow you up into a well-watered garden overflowing with the fruit of the Spirit.

90. Big Ducks on a Little Pond

"Press toward the mark…" Philippians 3:10-16; II Corinthians 3:18

    One bright and sunny spring morning, my husband and I gathered up our camera gear in preparation to go to one of our favorite places to shoot pictures. It is a beautiful arboretum located in the heart of our city. It has many lovely gardens, streams, waterfalls, and ponds which people can explore while walking on its trails. As we explored that morning, I came upon a delightful sight. There on the rocks, at the edge of a pond, sat a mother duck and her five little ducklings. They were in their fluffy and adorable stage, staying very close to their mother.

I am sure that from their point of view, the pond must have looked enormous, but as they got older and began to swim well, they explored more and more of it. When almost grown, they discovered that they could fly. Right about that time, they were feeling very confident like they were the rulers over that pond. They knew everything there was to know about it. They didn't need Mom at all.

Then one day, they were flying around and went farther than ever before. They were astounded to discover a huge lake, many times bigger than their pond, just across the road. There were other birds they never knew existed. Suddenly, they realized how small they really were and how much they still needed to learn.

Many of us get comfortable in our own little empires and get to thinking that we know all there is to know. We pray less and less because we've got this, and we don't need any help from God. That's God's favorite time to shake things up and humble us to remind us that we always need Him.

Always stay humble and teachable. We have not arrived until we get to Heaven. We always need to learn and grow. We are not invincible! Without the Lord in control, our empires would surely fall! There are bigger challenges yet to come and oceans of experience yet to be discovered.

www.ingramcontent.com/pod-product-compliance
Lightning Source LLC
Chambersburg PA
CBHW041543220426
43665CB00002B/24